Am I Not A Person?

Sylvia Hurt

A proportion of the royalties from the sales of this book will go to the Nottingham Rape Crisis Centre and The Bulwell Toy Library, Bulwell, Nottingham

Am I Not A Person?

Sylvia Hurt

First published by The Word Factory of Nottingham in 1998

The Word Factory
Syntax House
PO Box 186
Nottingham NG11 6DU

A CIP catalogue record for this book is available
from the British Library

ISBN: 0 9532051 0 X

Cover concept, title and blurb by Rory Baxter
Final design and artwork by Mono Design, Derby

Printed and bound in England by
The Bath Press, Bath

Contents

Foreword

There have been several books published on sexual abuse, with the vast majority written by professionals giving advice to abused people.

Undoubtedly, these can be helpful ... but the only person that can ever **truly** understand the horrific experience that is sexual abuse is the victim.

It is very difficult for these books, usually based on research carried out in the USA or Canada and originally published there, to reach someone experiencing the horrors of sexual abuse in a council estate in the East Midlands.

But before you read this book, there are a few points that you may not be aware of concerning sexual abuse.

Firstly, sexual abuse is not primarily about sex, it is about abuse. It is about power, control, and the humiliation and degradation of another human being.

Child abuse is probably mankind at its sickest and we are rightly horrified whenever we learn about it. In the main, we are shocked that somebody could do such a thing to a child, a totally defenceless and innocent child who looks to an adult for trust and unconditional love.

But we would be wrong if we concentrated exclusively on the 'child' aspect of the abuse. And we would be way off the mark if we thought for a moment that it was a childhood experience that might somehow fade away as time went by.

What is often not appreciated - and what this book highlights - is the long-term effect that abuse can have on a person. Many abused people choose to blank their experience out and 'get on' with their lives, but does it ever really go away?

Abuse changes the way a person sees everything, how they perceive the world and the people in it. It takes away valuable experiences that we all take for granted. And it steals time from a person's life that can never be returned.

The effects of abuse can take many forms. In Sylvia Hurt's case, it has shown itself in her refusal to appear attractive to others, especially men, which has led to a soul-destroying compulsive eating disorder.

AM I NOT A PERSON?

When people see Sylvia, all they see is a fat person who has 'let herself go'. They don't see someone who has been mentally scarred from childhood and is fighting a daily battle against what that abuse has done to her. To be honest, why should they? We cannot assume that everybody whose appearance does not conform to our own standards has had a sad childhood and been the victim of some terrible abuse. But maybe we could at least think for a second or two that there might be something more than what we see on the outside.

Some may say that many of Sylvia's observations in this book - for example she says she was showing the classic signs of an abused child and asks why nobody recognised them - benefit from hindsight and a modern-day outlook. But are we so sure that we would spot these signs today? How many abused and lonely children - and adults - are out there who either cannot communicate what they feel or are too terrified to speak out?

One important point worth remembering above all others is that abuse is something carried out by people who have a problem. Those who are put down, humiliated, molested and raped are not the problem. It is not their fault and they should never, **ever** feel guilty about what has been done to them. Standing up against abuse of any sort is often extremely hard but they should not allow these shallow people to transfer their worthlessness on to them.

Abuse is a vile practice that not only ruins lives but can sometimes even lead to death and everything possible should be done to stop it. That means speaking out ... every battered wife, husband or partner, everyone that is bullied, raped or abused, and everyone who knows these things are happening ... they must make their voice heard because silence only protects and encourages the abuser.

Many people who are abused remain silent for obvious and not so obvious reasons ... feelings of shame, disgust, embarrassment, even what they believe to be love.

Far too many remain victims for the rest of their lives and never express how they feel. Their deep-seated anger is often taken out on the wrong people and a destructive chain reaction can begin.

But Sylvia Hurt says she is no longer a victim ... she is a survivor.

As Sylvia puts it: "I find thinking about what happened to me

ii

disgusting and degrading. Nevertheless, I have to write about it. It is a way of cleansing my body and mind. This poison has been festering in me for too many years."

Writing the book, she says, "breaks my heart and sets the tears flowing. The pain is almost too much to bear but I have to do it. I have to cleanse my body of the cancer, the filth and the shame."

As well as helping herself, Sylvia hopes that going through this painful process of remembering and recounting events in frightening detail will help the tens of thousands of abused people who will not speak of their experiences to realise that the problem is not theirs ... indeed, it was never their fault.

We should always remember that victims of abuse are people first and foremost, people stripped of their self-respect and dignity. And nobody - but **nobody** - deserves to be treated this way by another human being.

Says Sylvia: "If this book can prevent just one more person from suffering the horrors of sexual abuse, it will have been worthwhile."

One final point. This book has not been 'ghost-written'. Sylvia Hurt is the genuine author and you will be reading her words and hearing her voice. And as she articulates her pain, ask yourself this: "How was this person ever described as 'not much above the level of sub-normality'?"

Rory Baxter
Editor
The Word Factory
Nottingham
January 1998

PS - Silence is the abuser's greatest ally. For anybody who wants to break free or just wants to talk, we have listed some contact details at the back of this book.

Publisher's notes:

1. Sylvia Hurt is not a pseudonym. However, for legal
reasons, most of the other names in this book have
been changed.

2. Where known, copyrights and credits have been included for
photographs or illustrations used in this book. However,
if anyone knows the source of an uncredited photograph
or illustration, please inform us and we will insert a credit
in the next imprint.

3. The Word Factory, Nottingham, is an independent publisher
that has been trading since January 1993. It is not affiliated or con-
nected in any way to any businesses with similar names that may
have been formed subsequent to that date.

4. We would like to say an extra special thank you to
Clive whose support made this book possible.
"You've got to do it."

This book is dedicated to my three children Lisa, Mark and Carl for giving me the strength to carry on in my darkest moments of despair.

Also, to the volunteers at Rape Crisis who gave me support and help with the pain of the past. They have helped me for many years and are still there for me.

I would also like to thank the senior social worker who prevented my kids being taken away from me forever, Isabella for helping me to express myself in art, and Charlotte the college tutor for all her help.

Finally, a big thank you to Rory, one of the few men I have been able to trust, for his hard work and his determination to bring the long-term effects of sexual abuse to a wider audience.

Chapter 1

A childhood?

We are so special,
That's what everyone says,
My twin and I.
Different in every way,
We are not identical.
Different as chalk and cheese
But we always wanted to please.
My twin, my twin was knocked from pillar to post
What it did to him no-one knows.

I was born into a very poor family of four brothers and one sister. The eldest child, Neville, was from my mother's first marriage.

Danny was next, followed by my twin John who was two minutes older than me. John and I weighed in at just two pounds each; we were always tiny twins. All through my childhood I was so thin and waif-like that I was known as Dainty Diana.

We lived in Stretton Street in St Ann's, a deprived area of Nottingham. Our house was a three storey terrace that was very unkempt … and so were we. Dad worked as a taxi driver but didn't earn very much.

Life there was very mundane and miserable but at times we did have some fun. I remember my friends and I would go up to Mapperley brickyard and collect red-crested newts to race. We'd also spend hours poking sticks into the rubbish, squealing as the rats jumped out.

When I think of Stretton Street now I can still smell the breast of lamb cooking in the oven and the Echo margarine melting in the pan of mashed potatoes.

Mum had an enormous task feeding the whole family and she would often solve the problem by mixing a can of tomatoes with lots of lard to make tomato dip. She would spread the margarine on the bread and submerge it in the dip. Mmmm.

Other memories of this time include Mum getting the 'bug

lady' in to check our house for damp. She was well known in the area for fumigating homes that were damp and had become ideal breeding places for bugs. Fortunately, our house passed her tests.

I also remember the rag man coming up the street to collect from the houses. We would give him some old bits and in return we would get a goldfish in a plastic bag. I used to ask Mum for some rags but she would never give me any. My friends always made sure I had enough for the rag man and in return I would give them my goldfish.

When Mum became pregnant for the fifth time, the rest of us were farmed out to various relatives. It was the practice. After a few weeks of being separated, we were all beckoned home. Mum had given birth to another son.

I suppose like all children that have been away from home for a while, I was looking forward to going back, especially to see John again in familiar surroundings.

But my happiness did not last long.

In all the excitement of being back home I had forgotten what a tough regime we had to stick to, forced on us by Dad, an ex-military police officer who was strict up to the point of being sadistic. He used to line us up to inspect our necks, ears and nails, and he would constantly yell at us and give us the belt, showing no mercy.

As for Mum, she was very academic and when out in public certainly knew how to put on the airs and graces. There was a definite refinement about her. But on the home front, she was entirely different. Even at a tender age, I recognised the rejection from her and knew that my Mummy didn't love me.

I remember I would try to climb on to her knee for some affection but I was always ushered away. I was told "Mummy's too busy", but she didn't seem to be doing anything important. I was always a bother and she looked at me with a scowl as if she really did hate me.

True, poverty and hardship were rife at the time, but it felt like Mummy almost delighted in making me look scruffy. John's clothes were clean but mine were always filthy.

I tended to be sick a lot as a child and was regularly at the doctor's on Nottingham's Mansfield Road with throat infections. To be honest, I found going to the doctor's quite pleasurable because he would talk to me in a caring way. I also loved the soothing lozenges and cough mixture that Mum got on prescription. When she unwrapped my lozenges and gave them to me she was paying me attention, which is all I wanted.

At the age of five we started school and I remember so vividly my first day at the Victorian Shelton Street school near Nottingham city centre.

As I walked along in my dingy socks and grubby coat, I decided to scream and dawdle [John had run on ahead]. I knew Mummy would shout at me but for a few seconds she would be giving me her undivided attention.

I remember once, when I arrived at school, snotty-nosed, cold and red-eyed, Mum took me to the cloakroom where the warmth hit me straight away ... the pipes around the room must have been on full. In contrast to how Mum treated me, the school felt so warm and friendly and there was always a nice smiling face to greet me.

Mummy left us and John was soon engrossed in the sandpit. But I just stood alone and began to cry.

The teacher looked concerned and as she bent down to comfort me I told her: "Mummy doesn't love me." But she just looked at me, took me over to where the other children were playing happily and left me. Nothing more was said.

I felt alienated and isolated. The other children all had nice, clean clothes and I knew I was different.

I ran over to John but he seemed to ignore me and was enjoying himself playing in the sand. I don't think he liked it when I clung on to him.

Before I knew it, it was time to go home. But even as the bell sounded for home-time, John just carried on playing.

I stood in the cloakroom, trying to be independent by putting my coat on by myself, when I saw Mummy coming towards me, scowling with a look of anger that told me again that she didn't love me.

John and I soon settled into the routine of school and enjoyed having the freedom to play. We really liked the school dinners and loved the puddings. But as the months went on, John and I would spend more and more time apart, each of us with our own friends.

And we would only see Dad at night because he would have to be up very early each day to go to work. When we did see him, John and I were always really scared.

AM I NOT A PERSON?

Mum paid Neville and Danny special attention. They were never smacked and our youngest brother - George - was never hit either.

One of my more pleasant memories was at bath-time on a Sunday afternoon, when Mum would boil the buckets of water and put the old tin bath in front of the fire. The first in had the clean water and the last one had to lie in all the muck and try to dry off with towels that were by then soaking wet.

After my bath I always felt fresh, especially if I got to go in first. And to top it off, I would have the old black oven plate wrapped in newspaper put into my bed to warm it up.

It was absolute heaven ... until I heard the bedroom door go.

I knew what was going to happen because it had happened so many times before. I knew it was Daddy before the shadow of his head peeped around the door.

"All right, ducky?" he always asked.

"Yes Daddy," I'd whisper.

Daddy felt different when he was in my bedroom. He seemed so kind and would talk to me in his soothing voice, not like the voice he used downstairs.

He would also give me a hard chocolate caramel, my favourite sweetie. I knew I was special and that no-one else knew about my treats. I had sweeties and my brothers had none, so I knew that Daddy loved me.

As I lay in bed he would gently touch my thin body, cuddling me and spending time on what I later learnt were my private parts. I had no idea what he doing but I loved the attention.

"Don't tell anyone," he would whisper as the hot air escaped from under the bedclothes.

"Daddy, don't move me," I'd whisper back as I began to get cold, then ask: "Why, Daddy?" when he told me again and again not to let on to anyone about what went on between us.

"Don't!" he'd snap and the sound of his voice told me to keep quiet as he pushed a couple more sweeties into my hand. I wouldn't have told anyone anyway, because if I did Daddy would use the belt and the thought of that alone paralysed me with fear.

By the time John and I had progressed to the juniors we were classed as children who were not academically good. We were always being told that we were "dunces".

The mental torment was taking its toll on both of us and we

4

could see no end to it. As well as Mum's rejection and the episodes at night with Daddy, even my step brother and brother would take turns being cruel to me.

I began to ask myself: "Why was I born?"

It was especially painful for me to watch the violence inflicted on John and it was beginning to affect his schooling. John and I could not concentrate for very long or spell very well. We were bottom in every subject and our older brothers would constantly taunt us about our inability to do simply tasks.

But the torment didn't end there. Every night after tea, John and I would be made to sit at the table in a routine that we loathed. Mother would put a list of words in front of us and we were allowed 10 minutes to memorise them before they were taken away.

She would then give us a pencil and paper and sit there telling us what words to spell. We knew we couldn't do them and the fear was too much for us. Many's the time John would wet himself because he knew that every word we spelt wrong meant a lash from the belt when Daddy came home.

I was petrified and the more I thought about the punishment the more answers I got wrong. And I knew that if we flinched when we were hit by the belt we would get another two strokes. Just remembering this now makes my eyes well with tears.

After we'd had the belt, Dad would come upstairs to see me in my bedroom. What he said and did then confused me so much that I began to think he had two heads ... a nice one and a horrible one.

As I lay in bed sobbing, my hands on fire, the door would open.

"I didn't mean it Syl," he'd whisper. "It's your Mum's fault."

Between my sobs I would glance up. The fondling had moved on a step further and Dad had begun to expose himself to me. I thought all Daddies did this. I suppose love is blind and I loved my Daddy so much. I saw no wrong in what he was doing and I knew I was his special little girl.

This kind of routine had been a part of my life since I was three and I had no reason to question it. But I knew that if I told anyone about it Daddy wouldn't love me anymore. I knew I would suffer rejection from him as well as from Mum and I couldn't take that. So it remained our secret.

And while the fondling and exposing continued from Dad, another member of the family introduced himself to me in a sexual manner, this time under threat. It was Neville. He was considerably older than me [I was five and he was 10].

Our house in Stretton Street had a front garden not much bigger than a postage stamp but I would often sit on the lawn to try to escape my tormentors, gathering rose petals with the aim of making perfume.

I didn't have many possessions but what I did have I treasured. One of my favourites was my dolls' house, made out of hardwood with windows made from cellophane.

One summer's day, I was playing out when I heard an almighty voice bellowing: "SYLVIA, IN!! ... SYLVIA, IN!!"

I immediately ran into the house and was suddenly whacked around the head by Neville.

"Where's your dolls' house?" he smirked.

"I don't know," I said in a sulk. After all, I had just been slapped around the head and I had no idea what for. As I continued to sulk he grabbed by bony arm and pulled my small body upstairs. My heart was racing and I began to feel breathless. The fear had paralysed my voice.

I knew that my step brother kept his pet mice in the attic in our house. But I was scared and I would never dare go up there. In fact, with the touching continuing from Daddy I rarely went upstairs on my own if I could help it.

We eventually reached the attic and he opened the door. There, right in front on me, was my prize possession, my beautiful dolls' house. I was confused and I started to cry. Not satisfied with his sexual abuse he had begun to use mental cruelty as well.

"It's mine now," he said with a smirk, and through my tears I could see that the windows had been taken out and replaced with wire mesh. And there, peering through the mesh was his family of mice.

I was heartbroken ... but there was no point telling Mummy and Daddy because I knew they wouldn't listen to me.

In this strange, almost Alice In Wonderland world, it wasn't long before we were all sitting around the table for tea, with me hurt and angry and liable to fly off the handle. Which is why I soon came to feel the heartless cruelty of my mother. The coldness I felt towards her at that time because of how she treated me is still with me today.

Even at such a young age, I would try to stop her being so cruel. I would get angry and answer her back when she called me "dunce". I knew I wasn't a dunce but it was fatal to argue with her.

I remember her coming over to me once, before I'd had even a mouthful of food, saying "Right, Diana" and pulling me towards the cellar. I pulled back but I knew she would win in the end.

She knew all too clearly how petrified I was of the dark but she didn't listen to my pathetic pleas for mercy. As the door shut and she slid the bolt into place, I collapsed on the cold cellar steps in the pitch blackness and sobbed into my hands.

Some time after, my hunger getting worse, I saw a chink of light coming through a grate at the bottom of the steps. Although every noise and shadow was like a monster to me, I moved towards the light and sat down on a slag heap near to the grid, still crying uncontrollably.

Between my sobs I heard a faint whisper: "Syl, Syl, quick, it's me." I knew it was John; he had smuggled some bits out of the kitchen and was pushing them through the grate for me. I couldn't speak and was still crying, but I was vaguely aware that John had gone almost as quickly as he'd appeared.

As I sat there wondering if/when I would be allowed back into the land of the living I heard my Mum and Dad raising their voices. Then I heard the familiar sounds of John being beaten. My twin was being thrashed because he tried to help me. Although he never cried while he was being hit, I was sobbing buckets.

For eight years of my life I suffered in silence. My only companion in my darkest moments was a small Dutch dolly with a pot face. Often, I would manage to grab her before I was shut away and many is the time she kept me company on those cold, hard steps.

The amount of time I stayed there ranged from a few minutes to several hours, but every time I emerged the table and the meals had been cleared away and I was ushered straight to bed, only to undergo a different kind of abuse. I kept asking myself when my nightmare would go away.

AM I NOT A PERSON?

I had made several friends at school and would chatter away, never daring to mention my dark secret and my miserable existence. Though I was hurting inside so badly, I constantly cried for John.

I was possibly nine or 10 when I noticed Mummy's tummy getting bigger, but nobody told me she was going to have another child. It was a terrible shock to me when she gave birth. I was ushered into the bedroom and there in an oak drawer was a new baby. Mum had called her Annie.

Once again, I was in emotional turmoil. Mummy loved the baby girl and I was heartbroken. The only thing I could cling to was my faithful companion, my little Dutch dolly.

But even this small comfort was to be taken away from me. One day, Danny was threatening me and wanting to do things I didn't want to do. I wouldn't give in to his lust and I put up a fight. So what did he do? He stamped on my dolly and broke her into pieces. I was devastated. Once again, I had had my favourite toy taken from me.

But he didn't stop there. As I knelt in the cobbled back yard, sobbing and trying against all odds to put the pieces back together, he stamped on her again.

"Please Danny, don't Danny!" I pleaded with him, begging him to mend her.

On another occasion, one of my tormenting brothers broke both my little fingers. The pain still haunts me today and the stunted growth of my fingers is daily testament to the cruelty they inflicted on me.

But nobody paid any attention. Mum was very busy with the new arrival and with running the home. I couldn't grasp how she could cuddle Annie but not John and me. Was there something wrong with us?

When Mum took Annie out, she left Neville in charge and my nightmare would begin again.

Not long after Mum had left, I would hear him beckon me back in to the house, even though John and Danny were in the street. The tone of his voice and the look in his eyes convinced me that I had to obey his every word, even though I knew what he was going to do to me.

When I entered the house I held my body against the wall and slowly slid by him. As I did, he grabbed my arm and pulled me up the stairs. I knew I had to obey when I saw the anger in his face and fear took hold of my frail body.

I was thrown on to the bed like a rag doll. There was no mercy shown. His hands explored every part of my body. He would be kissing me and pushing his tongue right into my mouth. I could feel his penis weeping on to my stomach.

As my small frame tried to stop this violation of my body and mind, he masturbated and ejaculated over my stomach. And after he had finished, I had the degrading and sickening task of wiping it away.

I felt unloved and physically sick, and this happened to me every time Mum went out.

I felt desperate but without a voice. And I felt worthless. After all, I had been told so many times that I was a dunce.

I remember so vividly shouting for Mummy between my sobs when I was shut in the cellar, but my voice went unheard. So how could I tell her now what was happening to me? I knew she didn't love me. I knew she wouldn't listen.

Bizarrely, there were also some happy times in my childhood, although very few of them are particularly memorable.

One pleasant memory concerns our holidays in Yorkshire. I always knew when we were going off to my dear Aunt and Uncle's, because all the gardens in the Nottingham area had gardens with daffodils in full bloom. We always went around Easter time and I knew when we were in Yorkshire I would be free from my torture.

I remember Mum would be busy packing and Dad would be trying to get the big American car into a reasonable condition to get us there ... and back!

Mum had filled the pop bottles up with water and Dad had loaded a box of one pence bags of crisps he had picked up from the Smiths warehouse. Mum would put a bottle of vinegar in her bag and some salt which she would sprinkle on later so we had our very own salt and vinegar crisps.

As we were all loaded into the car we were warned that any misbehaving and we would be thrown out. It scared me, and even though the boys were constantly bickering I didn't dare speak.

The trip to Yorkshire would take anything from three to four hours, depending on how the car was running. As we travelled along we all sang our seaside song because we knew that the holiday would include a day at Bridlington and Flamborough Head.

When we eventually arrived at the farm, Aunty Maud was there to greet us with a great big smile: "Hello Mary, get the bairns inside and let's give them some tea."

Their place was a typical farmhouse with plenty of clutter and loads of warmth. The coal fire would be burning furiously and Aunty would make us toast on a fork in front of the fire which we would eat later with scrambled fresh farm eggs.

Aunty had six children which made a total of 12 at meal times, needing two sittings to accommodate us all.

The fresh air and feeling of freedom I felt on the farm was wonderful to me. I used to get up bright and early so I wouldn't miss the chance to pick the farm eggs. At any one time, there was usually half a dozen of us collecting.

Uncle Ron would shout us in and greeting us would be the wonderful aroma of bacon and tomatoes and an enormous mug of tea each.

At bedtime, we all shared a huge mattress and were 'top and tailed' to make things easier. They say there's safety in numbers and they're right. I felt safer there than anywhere else on the planet. We used to have competitions painting hard boiled eggs and, although I never won, I loved the freedom of not being criticised.

When Mum packed up to come home, she had twice as much stuff as she had started with, this time loaded down with dozens of eggs and many other luxuries she couldn't afford to buy herself.

On our way back Dad used to stop and let us see the lighthouse at Flamborough Head. He would also take us to Bridlington, where the beach was so flat and the sea was lovely. But I knew in my heart that after this I would be returning to my tortuous existence.

I remember once we were on our way home and Dad had dished out the crisps. We were all extremely tired and it wasn't long before we were all asleep. But Dad soon woke us up: "Here kids, get this gum chewed ..."

Apparently, the car had sprung a leak somewhere and he needed to bung the hole to get us home. The car managed to get us to the forest and for the last leg Mum got us all on to a bus. I can't remember to this day what happened to the car.

AM I NOT A PERSON?

The holiday in Yorkshire was wonderful and I wished it would last forever. But Aunty didn't know what I was going through and fear stopped me telling her. The piercing eyes of my abusers were haunting me all the time.

I also had many happy experiences visiting my other Aunt in the Meadows area of Nottingham. She used to show me an enormous amount of love and affection and I will always be grateful to her for that. I treasure these memories because for two wonderful weeks I was free from my living hell.

Aunt Meg was very poor but always catered for anyone arriving on her doorstep. Once a week I would turn up with Mum's washing and go to the wash house with her. Even at such an early age, I was conscious of the state of Mum's dirty washing. The towels resembled floor cloths!

There were iron sinks with scrub boards and hot water as well as a penny ironing machine and huge drying racks. The fresh and clean smell of the clothes drying was something I was not used to.

On Friday afternoons I would get out my dear Aunty Meg's coach built pram and we would make the 20-minute walk to Wilford Road pit to fill it with coal. I knew the routine and would ask excitedly: "Shall we get the pram out, Aunty?" I also knew how lovely it was when the fire was roaring in her old terraced house.

"Yes Sylvia," she would say, "but mind you don't hurt yourself."

I was always keen to please Aunty and I would haul the huge pram out of the coalhouse. She would then lay her candlewick bedspread and curtains in the bottom of the pram.

As I skipped along I would suck my frozen Jubbly that Aunty had bought for me and her two children. I was really happy and for a short time I felt like a normal child.

When we arrived at the pit top I was first to start loading the pram. My cousins would join in and within minutes the pram would be almost overloaded with coal.

Aunty would fasten the bedspread and curtains around the load so there were no spillages and we would make our way back, which seemed to take an age. But we got there eventually.

When we arrived, Aunty would poke the fire and it would roar. She had left the corned beef stew simmering while we

11

were out and I was looking forward to the peas, potatoes, onions, corned beef and Oxo gravy thickened with flour.

As I sat there staring into the fire I wanted to tell Aunty about my abuse but I didn't dare. Again, the fear stopped me. The consequences of me speaking out were too serious and I knew I would be dead if I ever told.

I classed Aunty Meg's house in Hartford Street as my home and I made many friends there. In the school holidays my friends and cousins would walk to Trent Bridge and around the Victorian rock gardens. We would take our socks off and get soaked in the paddling pool. It was all free and we loved it. When we were hungry we would eat the bread, margarine and crisps that Aunty had packed for us and drink our bottles of frozen water she had given us. As we walked back we would play games.

When we arrived at Aunty's tired and thirsty, she would give us all a frozen Jubbly which we'd suck while sitting on the kerb.

One summer's night on one of our memorable holidays at Aunt Meg's, we were playing hopscotch and marbles when we heard the sound of drums and trumpets playing down the street. All six of us ran to see where the music was coming from. It was the Salvation Army, they always toured the streets in our area. We just stared in awe, listening to the wonderful music.

I looked longingly at one of the female officers who had ruddy cheeks and a bonnet-type hat with a huge rosette on it. Her happiness showed in her face for everybody to see.

Then she started to sing and a voice shouted: "Come on children, join in!"

Jesus wants me for a sunbeam
A sunbeam, a sunbeam
I will be a sunbeam for him ...

I began to wonder if Jesus wanted me for a sunbeam. Maybe he would help me to be the same as the other children in the area with nice clothes, nice toys and happiness. After all, a sunbeam is bright and beautiful. The abuse would go away and Mummy would love me.

Jesus sounded just the person I had been looking for. After this experience I would constantly sing "Jesus wants **me** for a sunbeam!" and ask my friends to help me to look for Jesus.

AM I NOT A PERSON?

They just laughed and taunted me, asking: "Have you found Jesus yet, Sylv?"

One Sunday evening while at Aunty Meg's, I asked my friends if they would come with me to Jesus' house. Again they laughed, so I skipped along Arkwright Street towards St Saviours church on my own. As I sang that I wanted Jesus with me, I stopped and looked down at my appearance.

"You don't mind me coming to your house dirty do you, Jesus?" I asked, expecting a reply. But there was just an eerie silence. I walked up the drive of the church, hoping Jesus would appear and buy me some nice clothes.

Standing on my toes and peering in I saw there was a service in full swing, with everybody dressed in their Sunday best. I slid into the church and sat at the back.

Then I knelt down and said: "You're not cross with me for having old clothes on are you Jesus?" but he still didn't answer and I thought that he must be very cross with me.

As I sat back on the seat I was desperately looking for Jesus to tell him I would definitely be a sunbeam for him. I also wanted to ask him to tell Mummy off for not loving me.

Then someone passed a bowl to me with money in it. I said "I can't lend Jesus any money" and people just stared at me then took the bowl away. After sitting and waiting for a while I knew Jesus wasn't going to come to see me so I left the church.

Skipping back to Aunty's, I said: "You didn't talk to me Jesus, did you? You don't love me either," and when I arrived I told Aunty I had been to Jesus' home. She looked at me and gave me a gentle smile.

The next day, I called for my friends and told them where I'd been and they all burst out laughing. I was disillusioned about Jesus and not looking forward to going back home.

When I was 10, Aunty asked me if I wanted to join the Brownies and I asked: "Will I see Jesus?"

"No," she said quite seriously, "you will see Brown Owl."

Aunty took me and I did meet Brown Owl, who sorted out a smart brown uniform for me and made me a fully fledged Brownie. I wore that uniform with pride and looked forward to talking to Jesus every Sunday parade. I still thought Jesus would rescue me from the torture I was going through.

I knew that when this holiday was over I had a lot of school work ahead and some major changes. Mum had decided that I

13

should attend Sycamore Secondary Girls' School and we had already been to have a look around. I liked what I saw but I didn't understand why John and I were to be separated. It was like losing one of my limbs.

My first day arrived and even though I was a little nervous I soon made some friends. I was a chatty child but never once breathed a word of my secret life at home.

However, my school life was a pretty miserable existence because I was continually taunted with my inability to keep up with the work. Except for Physical Education, I was bottom in every subject. I was called a dunce again and my nickname was 'Scruffy Sylvia'. My uniform was always dirty and at times it wasn't even the regulation clothing.

Most families in the area were poor and a lot of the girls had second-hand clothes but they were clean and well turned out. When I was taunted I felt angry at Mum, especially since the boys went to school looking smart.

The two questions spinning around my head all the time were why didn't Mum care about me and what had I done?

Dad always cut our hair and his military experience showed. So here I was in what should be the most important years of my life, looking and feeling like some kind of freak.

Because schools in the inner cities were renowned for having a lot of children from poor families, they would often arrange holidays for some of the kids. I was thrilled when I was picked with several other girls out of my class. The holiday was all paid for and all we had to find was adequate clothing and a little spending money.

I didn't care that I wouldn't have many clothes. I would be away from the dark secrets for three whole weeks!

We were each given letters for our parents in brown envelopes, stating that we needed to have a medical. Mum took me along and I was scared when I got into the room where several other children were waiting.

My name was called and we were shown into a room. I found myself in front of a stocky woman dressed in a white overall. As I looked up I noticed two huge moles sticking out of her face and long grey hairs growing out of them.

When she started to check my teeth I wet myself. She scolded me for it and told me to stand up straight in a stern voice. She then dipped a comb in Dettol and checked my hair for lice.

AM I NOT A PERSON?

After checking my feet and a few other bits she said I was germ-free and fit to go.

Mum gave me the set amount of spending money and Dad dropped me off at the meeting place in Huntingdon Street in central Nottingham. The atmosphere was electric with excited children talking happily while waiting for the coaches.

Teacher did the roll call and before I got on the bus Mum bent over to kiss me goodbye. I took the kiss off my cheek and put it in my heart. I was so pleased and as I sat at the back of the coach I whispered to my friend: "I'm never going to wash my cheek, I don't want to wash Mummy's kiss away."

We were all given name tags to pin on our coats and another check was made to make sure everyone was on board. Then we were on our way! Not long after the coaches pulled away from the back-to-back houses our teachers got us singing, stopping half-way for a toilet break and a 10-minute wander.

The holiday home we were going to was called Roseberry House and I visualised it in my mind with pretty gardens and rambling roses. Before we knew it [many of us had dozed off], our teacher told us we would soon be arriving, adding that we had to stand in single file when we got off the coach and await our instructions.

As the coach pulled in, a shocking image hit me. The home looked like some kind of prison with huge fences all around. The place looked quite dull and unappealing.

When we had all lined up, an 'Uncle' appeared [the people who were in charge were called Uncles and Aunties], led us into the home and showed us our dormitories. We were then assembled to have our heads checked for head lice again and told to have a shower before tea was served. Already, I hated it! Torture at home and now this. These disadvantaged children had been duped and were at the mercy of total strangers. Although I couldn't express it at the time, in my mind I felt we were so vulnerable to the evils of the world and it seemed like another form of abuse.

At meal times I'd distance myself from everyone and begin to feel alone again. Even though several girls had come from my school, most of my friends were back in Nottingham. I wanted to run away.

Everything at Roseberry House was done in an orderly way. We had a few hours' schooling and were allowed some time in the play area. And after a few days, we were even escorted to the cinema.

At night time we were ushered to our beds and Uncle brought us our bread and dripping for supper. This was the most pleasurable thing about the holiday because I loved dripping with jelly and salt.

The food killed the pain for a while but I needed someone to talk to. My body felt like a tightly twisted coil. And although we were often taken to the beach which passed some time, I couldn't wait to get back on the coach and see my dear Aunt Meg and my friends again.

At last, the day came to leave and we all boarded the coaches and, as usual, I sat at the back. Most of us had bought presents when we were taken shopping. I had spent my money on an ornament for Mummy.

Throughout this whole period, my head felt as if it was going to explode. I desperately wanted to talk to someone to rid myself of the shame and pain of my secret world. I wanted to be happy and like the other children but, above all, I wanted Mummy's love.

Mum was there to meet me when we arrived but she looked cross. I had seen this face so many times and it made me sad. I gave her the present which she put straight into her bag then dragged me to the car. I knew she was cross because I had come home.

Within a few months of being home, the cruelty and the abuse began to take its toll again. I couldn't concentrate on anything at school, not even to copy off the blackboard. I tried so very hard but I just couldn't do it.

Because of how we performed, there were discussions about John and me going to a special school. I begged Mum to let me stay at Sycamore and pleaded my case with my form teacher. Thankfully, they agreed.

I remember the times I would stand in the playground trying to memorise my work but it just wouldn't stay in my head, even the really simple stuff.

The teachers took turns to do playground duty and I liked it when Mrs Clough the PE teacher - my favourite - was there [I was really good at netball, hockey and tennis]. She cared about me and took time to talk to me as if I was equal to the other children.

AM I NOT A PERSON?

On one of our little chats, she told me it was the Red House's turn to read in assembly and that she thought I was the right girl to read the lesson from the bible. "Me!?" I squealed. I couldn't believe it.

Mrs Clough said she would help me to get it right and spent 10 minutes with me after school for two weeks. I felt proud; I was so pleased that this teacher had faith in me. She knew I was an intelligent pupil and definitely not 'backward', a word I had heard people say so many times.

Until my dying day I will be grateful to Mrs Clough. The psalm I used to read to her every night in the classroom is embedded in my mind forever.

I will lift up mine eyes unto the hills
From whence cometh my help
My help cometh from the Lord ...

I was thrilled when I had it word-perfect two days before the assembly but in my heart I knew my appearance would let me down. I desperately wanted to look clean and I had asked Mummy several times if I could wash my uniform. She gave me a stern "No!" each time, which is what I had expected, but it didn't stop me trying.

When the day arrived, I was determined that if I couldn't have a nice uniform I was definitely going to have shiny shoes. I got up earlier than usual to polish them, but they still looked shabby and I felt as scruffy as ever.

Even though nobody wished me luck, I was so proud of myself because someone had recognised my capabilities. As I made my way to school, saying the psalm over and over in my mind, I was so thrilled that I had a bounce in my step. I felt good because I genuinely wanted to please and here was a real chance. But while I walked I glanced down at my uniform and couldn't help but feel ashamed.

I got to school 10 minutes early as arranged and was greeted by Mrs Clough.

"How nice to see you," she smiled and took me into her office. "Here you are love, try these on."

In her arms was a neatly pressed full school uniform, including nice clean socks. I was so excited I dashed into the toilets to change. In each sink there was a bar of red carbolic soap and I washed by grubby hands and face so much they seemed to shine.

AM I NOT A PERSON?

I quickly put on my nice, crisp blouse and uniform and looked in the mirror. I shone like a new penny, clean and bright. When I left the toilet I felt equal for the first time since joining the school. I was filled with immense pride.

Mrs Clough took me to my spot on the stage and within minutes the assembly began. When I looked up, head held high, I saw my PE teacher's caring eyes. I took a deep breath and read the psalm, my voice quivering with emotion.

When I'd finished and stepped down from the stage, I knew then that I wasn't thick or stupid and I was so pleased I had been given the chance to prove it.

My pride lasted for precisely one hour while I wore that clean uniform, but the feeling will live in my memory forever.

Later that day, the class was made to stand and as we started to sing a chink of sunlight shone into the room.

Now the day is over, night is drawing nigh
Shadows of the evening steal across the sky ...

I had a few happy times at school playing jacks and marbles and for a while I would push my 'other world' to the back of my mind. Everybody was totally unaware of my pain, of the shadows and the smells that dominated my life.

Even though our area was renowned for its poverty, there were plenty of places to play. Colwick Woods was within walking distance of St Ann's and Bath Street Park, close to Sneinton Market, was even nearer. I considered Bath Street Park to be my garden of freedom, where I could escape from my torture.

But the abuse continued to affect my school work and by the age of 12 I was regularly playing truant. I would walk through Robin Hood Chase, a Victorian park lined with laburnums and huge elm trees. I especially liked walking there in the rain. The different earthy smells from the ground and rain splashing on my face gave me a sense of freedom. Not only did I enjoy the solitude when staying off school, but I loved exploring the majesty of Mother Nature.

Although I felt in a way that it was destroying my body and soul, I still thought nature was wonderful. The flowers in every well-kept garden I walked past were glorious and for a while helped me to forget the terrible people in my life.

My many walks took me to the Shakespeare Street arboretum, which in itself is a wonderful place. It included Chinese gardens with cannons placed at the top of the hill and sometimes I would visualise these huge guns destroying my family.

At winter time, dressed in totally inadequate clothing for the weather, I would sit on a bench with the crisp white snow all around me, watching the blue tits and robins fighting for scraps of food. And I would just stare into the distance, with the lovely white snow flakes twisting and turning. At times they looked like crystals shining through a white blanket.

I would be frozen but Mum never knew. By now, I had lost all interest in school work and I couldn't get any lower .. mentally or physically.

Nobody picked up what was happening to me. They never asked, they just classed me as being retarded. I was being absent from school more and more and I was worried that Mum would find out. But the pain would be no different to any other day ... the belts, the horrible torture from everyone except John.

When I was 13 and Mum told me we were on the move to a place called Kimberley, it might as well have been halfway around the world. I knew I wouldn't be any happier there because my abusers would be moving with us. I simply couldn't see an end to my torture.

Mum was moving us into a shop-fronted place with a bathroom in it, very up-market compared to the old terrace. She had taken me to see it and I was struck by the enormous garden which had a shed and a coal heater in it. Within days, Mum and Neville had organised the removals van and we were on our way.

There was a lot I wasn't sure of at this stage, but what I did know was that I would be going to a mixed school, which meant John and I would be together again.

I knew John had felt lost without my company and I felt the same. We had so much in common, including both being left-handed, but we were forced to use our right hands. John was quite stubborn at times and resisted and is still left-handed. To this day, I still use my right even though I find it easier to use my left.

Mum and Dad had sorted the basic furnishings out after a few days. The settee was propped up on bricks but at least we had a home [I've never criticised Mum and Dad for being poor]. Dad managed to get a reasonable job as a driver on Trent Buses, earning good money although the hours were unsociable.

I have good and bad memories about Kimberley. The most terrifying aspect of life there for me was the cellar … the dark cellar which will remain in my brain forever. The most pleasant memory is the book Little Women. I would read this favourite over and over in the garden shed which I had made 'my room', although the boys also chose it as their gang's meeting place.

Even at Kimberley, the abuse continued. They had full control of my body and mind and by now just the sight of Neville would make me freeze.

Since moving to Kimberley, Neville got a girlfriend who was still at school. But this didn't stop the terrible abuse and mental cruelty he was inflicting on me, such as making me wash the dishes in cold water with the grease floating on top. Feeling a little braver, I had started to answer him back but it made no difference.

"Please, I can't wash them," I pleaded.

"Get them done!" The tone of his voice convinced me that I had to do as I was told.

Some Sundays, Mum would make her special layer cake - a chocolate sponge with vanilla - and would serve fruit coated in Carnation milk. One time, she invited Neville's girlfriend over for tea and I knew that I would not be allowed to taste such luxuries. For some reason, I would be shut on the stairs while Neville's girl tasted the special cake. Why? Was I some kind of freak or perhaps a threat? Were they frightened of what I might say in front of a 'stranger'?

"Please, Neville," I would sob, "can I come down?"

There was never a reply. Yet again, my voice went unheard.

After the company had gone, the table was cleared and the food put away. Only then was I let off the stairs, only to be sent to bed soon afterwards without any tea.

After a week or so, John and I were to start at our new school - Kimberley Secondary School. George had enrolled at Gilt-brook School.

After the cruelty at home, I was eagerly looking forward to our first day at school. "A new start," I thought, although in my heart I knew I would never be academic or accepted by anyone. It seemed inevitable that I would play truant and miss school but I quite enjoyed the first few weeks because John was with me.

By now, Mum had made several friends on our road, which included quite a few and some big detached houses. In one of these lived an elderly man called Mr Carter who had given Mum some of his prized cooking apples and told her that if she needed any more she should send her lovely daughter up for them.

I remember arriving home from school one day to be told: "Diana, go to Mr Carter's for some apples."

I didn't mind going. I would do anything to get out of the house of horrors ... but my enthusiasm did not last long.

As Mr Carter went into his storage shed to get the apples, he began to touch me, mainly on my bust which had started to develop. Why was this man in his sixties fondling my young body? It was as if I had a label stuck on my forehead that said "please touch me".

No matter where I went, I could not escape the violation of my body and mind. Was I to blame for having an attractive body? I must have been doing something to make these people cause me so much pain. My faith in human nature was totally shattered and I developed a paranoia about meeting people. I was even scared of the open fields surrounding the house and absolutely petrified of the dark.

As I walked home with Mum's apples, I began to think of her as wicked. Did she know? After dropping the apples on the table, I made my way to the garden shed where I burst into tears. I felt such shame and hated myself so much that I started punching myself and sticking a knob pin into my arms.

Suddenly, the shed door opened and the two monsters - Danny and Neville - stood there. The look in their eyes told me they were going to hurt me and my heart began to race. My whole body was shaking and I couldn't swallow because the fear had paralysed my throat.

"Right, Diana, look what we've got." They held up 10 cigarettes, took one out and ordered me to smoke it. They knew that cigarettes disgusted me; Mum and Dad smoked and I hated it.

I felt so sick and my stomach began to ache.

"I can't," I sobbed, "I can't smoke any more!"

But they showed me no mercy and made me smoke all 10.

AM I NOT A PERSON?

I felt incredibly ill and frightened as I walked up to the house holding my stomach and crying. Mum heard me being sick but showed no sympathy.

"Diana," she said, "if you're ill you can go to bed."

I walked slowly up the stairs, sobbing. I needed Mum so much, but what had I done to be denied her love?

"Oh Mum, please ...," I whimpered.

Before I could say any more, she came rushing up the stairs, grabbed me and made me sit on the bed. Then she left the bedroom and shut the door. It's just as well she didn't stay because I didn't dare tell her why I was feeling sick. All I wanted was a bucket or something to be sick in.

But despite this, I liked the shed; it had became my home and I sewed and knitted in there on many occasions.

One day, as I sat there enjoying the peace and space, Neville and Danny came in and made me stand up. When I did, I noticed Neville's penis was out and I was scared. Danny held my head over it while Neville masturbated and ejaculated into my mouth. I can still taste it to this day and it sends a shiver through my bones.

Their coldness and control over me seemed like it would never end.

The fields surrounding our house were a haven for the average child and when Mum and Dad wanted some peace they would send us out to play in them. On one occasion, John and George had disappeared on one of their boys' adventures, which seemed exciting. It didn't take the abusers long to realise that they could take advantage of the situation.

Neville pushed me to the ground and began his sick routine ... this time in broad daylight. I froze with terror, just looking at the sky and hoping it would all end quickly. In a nearby tree, I saw Danny, staring at us with a sickening grin on his face.

What little dignity I possessed had now been completely taken away from me and my childhood was being stolen as well. I wanted to scream and I wanted to die. To face these monsters day in and day out was torture of the worst kind.

But was I to blame?

Chapter 2

A life down under

Hip hip hooray,
I feel free today.
We're on our way to a great
big liner berthed at Tilbury Docks.
Four weeks on board,
We're on our way to Oz.
A new start for me
Where I can gain some dignity
From the hurt and shame of the past.
I hope it will last.

One day, when I was nearly 14, Dad and Mum sat the family down and told us once again that we were to move house.

But it wasn't a move down the road this time or even to another part of the country ... we were going to Australia. Dad had got a job 'down under' and to him it was a chance not to be missed. His qualifications and work experience had passed the immigration authorities' strict requirements.

This was literally unknown territory for all of us! For us as kids the idea of travelling on a liner [as £10 immigrants] for four whole weeks was very exciting. To me, it seemed like a dream ... there would be no more school, no more degradation and no more humiliation. I couldn't wait!

For the next few weeks it was all I could think of. A new life, a new beginning. All my hopes for happiness were resting on us getting to Australia.

While we kids let our minds and conversations run wild with imagination, Mum busied herself packing what few belongings we would be taking.

Dad tidied up the rest of his affairs and after what seemed like a lifetime we were into our final week of living in England.

Before we could leave, though, the whole family had to have a medical. We passed with flying colours, except for Mum who had a gum disease and had to have all her teeth removed. She passed the second check and we were soon to be on our way!

AM I NOT A PERSON?

The night before we were leaving England for good, the kids were once again bundled off to stay with relatives. I went to stay with my Aunt who had shown me friendship and understanding. I would miss her deeply, so I made the most of the evening talking with her and trying to act as normal as possible. I knew saying goodbye was going to be heartbreaking.

While we were all farmed out, Dad had arranged to meet his mates in the Rifleman pub in The Meadows to bid a fond farewell to them all. Mum was going around to the neighbours and catching up on any gossip that she may have missed during her busy last few weeks.

Aunty told me I had to get up at the crack of dawn and be ready for when the rest of the family arrived at her house. Everyone turned up on time and we were each given something to carry. We did exactly as we were told without so much as a grumble. We all made our way to the Midland train station near Nottingham city centre. It was to be second class travel to Tilbury Docks.

I had never been on a train before but as excited as I was it wasn't long before the movement of the carriage sent me off into a world of dreams.

I woke when we arrived at Tilbury Docks and my eyes nearly popped out of my head, as did the rest of the family's. In front of us was an enormous P&O liner built in the 1930s, with what I think was SS Stralhaird painted on its side. This was to be our home for four weeks and who knew what would be in store for us after that?

When we'd boarded, all the children made their way to the top deck to see the start of the journey. The launching of the boat was a sight I will never forget, with our relatives on the docks saying their farewells.

After a few days, I thought I was in heaven. The journey was fabulous and we had three course meals ... not neck of lamb or dripping sarnies.

The sun seemed to be shining all of the time, although I'm sure it wasn't. But the excitement dimmed our vision of the weather ... it simply wasn't important. There were so many other things to do and I remember standing in awe then screaming loudly as I watched flying fish landing on the deck of the ship when crew members threw scraps overboard for passing whales! The liner was like our own little town.

We stopped at several ports on the way, including Cairo where Dad wanted us to disembark. He had been based there during his service in the military police and he wanted to show us where he did his training. But this was the one place where we were not allowed to leave the ship. The Suez Canal conflict had just started and for our own safety we were confined to the liner.

So we spent many hours in the swimming pool because Mum and Dad's budget was limited and they couldn't afford ice lollies and this was the next best way to keep cool. When we approached the equator we were all pushed into the swimming pool and given a certificate to mark the occasion.

I couldn't believe it ... I was experiencing more freedom than I had ever known. No abuse ... my body had become my own for the first time in a very long time. Maybe this was because we were all in such close confinement and the monsters would be found out if they tried anything.

Finally, our passage came to an end and as we disembarked I felt a pang of sorrow. I had enjoyed myself so very much and now I faced uncertainty of where my life was going. After we had all left the ship we were met by officials then taken to hostels by coach. We went to a huge complex not far from Melbourne which was used to house newly arrived immigrants.

The accommodation was very basic but it catered for our needs. The food was still of a high standard and I had no problem in eating seconds if there were any on offer. I had never had such luxuries. I remember turning on the radio and hearing Del Shannon singing Runaway. It wasn't so long ago that I'd wanted to be just that, a runaway. Now I was happy!

Within weeks of being in the hostel Mum and Dad were offered a former vicarage near St Kilda [Dad had taken us all to Australia through the Church of England scheme]. The house was set in its own grounds with verandas and fruit trees. At night I would watch the possums climbing the trees ... the place seemed like heaven.

The family appeared to be comfortable financially and I had made many friends. I think our Pommie accents were quite entertaining to the Aussies!

We went to church regularly and Dad had several friends in the congregation. One of them visited our house many times

AM I NOT A PERSON?

and I found out later that he ran a business of his own.

At the age of 14, I was interested in finding work and was thrilled when Dad arranged an interview with this friend. I was totally overjoyed when I got the job ... it didn't have great career prospects but it was money and after a few weeks I was able to buy myself the things I needed and wanted [within reason, of course].

On one morning, I was getting myself ready for work when there was a knock at the front door. Mum answered it and yelled up to me: "Diana, are you having a lift today?"

I knew that I hadn't made any arrangements, so I trotted downstairs to see who it was, dressed in my olive green dress and black peep toe shoes.

There was my boss. "Do you want a lift, Sylvia?" he said and I gladly accepted. Well, I thought, it isn't everybody who gets a lift to work from their boss! What a thoughtful man.

He opened the car door and I sat in the front, happy in the thought that I would be in work within 20 minutes. After a few minutes I looked around and realised we weren't going the way I expected.

"Where are we going?" I said, thinking innocently that we might be picking something up before going on to work. But as soon as I looked at him my heart began to pound. Fear gripped me because I had seen that look so many times in the past. He drove on without uttering a word and I began to fear for my life. When the car came to a sudden halt near the sea I yelled: "Where are we!? Where are we!?!" but he just lunged towards me and said: "Get out!"

I obeyed. I knew this man was in control of my body and mind. He dragged my waif-like frame towards some huge boulders and my skin crawled. Despite the intense heat, I felt cold all over. He flung me against the boulders and started to undress me.

"Don't! Don't!" I screamed but he quickly had me naked and stood there ogling every part of my body.

The crash of the waves killed my screams and cries as this man forced himself upon me. When he penetrated my vagina I let out an almighty scream. But he was controlling me now and I didn't dare move.

The pain I experienced was like a stabbing that seemed to last for hours but it was probably all over in seconds. When he'd finished, he stood back and I remember looking down and seeing his penis with my blood on it. It's an image that will stay with me forever.

My head and whole body felt like they would explode but as I sobbed he ordered me to get dressed and I obeyed immediately, repeating: "I'm bleeding, I'm bleeding ..."

He handed me something that seemed to resemble Vaseline but I was in no condition to understand how to use it. As I struggled to the car I felt I'd had all of my dignity stripped from me. He started the engine and I just stared into the distance. I couldn't believe that my boss had calculated this nightmare but he had clearly planned to rape me.

As we drove along there wasn't a word spoken. There wasn't anything I could say, anyway. I felt numb all over. He drove me back to my house and when we arrived he coolly told Mum that I had been ill at work. Then he drove off.

I must have had about 20 showers that day. I felt so dirty and worthless. Also, the thought of seeing him every day nearly sent me mad but I decided I would carry on with my job and keep another dark secret.

The abuse had even followed me to Australia! Surely it **had** to be my fault. Or had Dad told him what he had been doing to me, I wondered?

Now I just couldn't cope. I became a withdrawn individual and spent many hours alone, scrubbing myself to get rid of this filth. I started to eat and eat but my body remained slim and attractive.

Dad enjoyed his work at the docks but before long he was at home more and more because he had become a very sick man.

Then we all had the shock of our lives ... within 18 months of arriving in Australia we were preparing for our return to England. Dad had developed a heart complaint due to the strain of his job and he decided to take us all back 'home'. He knew he didn't have long to live and he was reluctant to leave Mum in a country she didn't know. Before we left, one of Dad's friends decided to take us all to the Luna Park fair with everything paid for. It was wonderful.

Dad's company had agreed to pay the £1000 it would cost to bring us all back to England as part of a compensation deal. It wasn't long before we were once again at Melbourne Docks, loaded with bags.

AM I NOT A PERSON?

This time we took a Dutch liner which I think was called the SS Zunderamine, built sometime in the '50s. After a while I was a little disillusioned because we were on a low deck and the food was not to the standard we'd had on our way out to Australia. In fact, it was foul.

Dad's health deteriorated rapidly while on the liner and he had to receive treatment from the ship's doctor. Mum carried on as normal … I suppose she had to for our sakes.

On one of our ports of call we had a tour around Naples. Money was still short but we got immense pleasure out of all the wonderful sights.

The trip back was very different to the one going out. It seemed to have a black cloud hanging over it. There was no fresh start to look forward to and I had felt a lot better in Australia because the abuse had stopped, even though when Dad looked at me he still undressed me with his eyes. But now we were going back to square one.

Chapter 3

Homeless in hell

What is a Dad?
A monster in my eyes.
I can't think of anything nice.
It makes me so sad.
Only the lust of someone who was sex mad

When we arrived in Nottingham it was a miserable, cold, damp day. Dad had arranged with relatives to find emergency accommodation for all of us and we were once again sent off to different houses. Except for Annie, who stayed with Mum and Dad at a flat Dad's friend had found on Mansfield Road. Once again, I stayed at my Aunt Meg's terraced house on Hartford Street.

Not that long ago, I had been working in Australia and it was a real shock to the system to have to return to school. Before I was due to start at Trent Bridge school, Dad paid me a visit. He looked gaunt and extremely ill. He had brought me a uniform Mum had sent which was totally inadequate for school ... but I knew she had a lot on her plate. The visit was very brief and Dad was soon on his way.

It was 1962 and I had been at my dear Aunt's some months. The summer soon arrived. A friend had given me a bicycle and I was mending a puncture at the back of the house when Mum appeared at my Aunt's front door. The first thing she said was: "Where's Diana?"

I dropped what I was doing and ran indoors. Mum was now in the living room and Annie was tugging at her skirt. I couldn't believe it, Mum was paying *me* a visit!

My excitement soon disappeared. "Pop's dead," Mum said. I looked at her and there was no emotion. That coldness was still there. I was so shocked that I ran out and rode off on my bike.

My mind was in a whirl ... I really couldn't work out my emotions. I felt sorry for Mum but I knew she didn't love me so I didn't try to cuddle her. I couldn't face the rejection. I know I loved Dad for the wrong reasons but I had lost the only person that hadn't neglected me. After his death, I stayed at my Aunt's but the abuse followed me there as well. Sometimes I would wake to find my Uncle in bed with me! The Aunt I loved so much clearly knew nothing about this.

I wanted to scream but who could I talk to?

My Aunt's brother-in-law, Stan, was a regular visitor ... he always called on Mum to see if she was okay. After all, my Mum had been married to his brother who had been killed in the war.

Stan had always shown an interest in me, buying me clothes, taking me swimming and buying me food. He even touched my body while I was in his care aged 15. I'd hardly been back in England long and I was being abused by my Uncle and now by my Aunt's brother-in-law.

It seemed every male that saw my body wanted to touch it. I began to feel extremely angry and was constantly asking questions. But Stan always bought me food which anaesthetised my pain.

Mum was always at the back of my mind. How was she managing without Dad? And it still hurt that she didn't want John and me. I began to question why she hadn't had us adopted if she disliked us so much. My mind was whirling round with a mix of emotions - anger, shame, worthlessness and pity.

What on earth had I done that was so bad for Mum not to want me? Oh, Mum, my arms were reaching out but you weren't there. I would have done anything for your acceptance of me. I know I wasn't perfect, but I was your daughter.

By this time, my food intake had become enormous. I began to eat constantly ... chips, crisps, chocolates. But I still had the body beautiful and I hated it. I didn't want another man to ogle my body. I just couldn't take any more abuse ... but how could I stop it and who could I turn to?

Once again, I went home to Mum's and once again the rejection, mental cruelty and abuse started. My brain felt as if it was going to burst out of my head. I knew that what was happening to me was definitely wrong but fear, those eyes and the tone of voice stopped me uttering a single word.

By 16, I lost control completely. I couldn't concentrate on holding a job down. I would last a couple of weeks but soon I'd be off, wandering around the streets of Nottingham, spending

AM I NOT A PERSON?

many an hour sitting in 'Slab Square'. I was homeless, hungry and a very angry and confused young woman.

I remember one time when I walked to the toilets at the side of the square, desperate to be clean and to feel like a normal teenager. Oh, how I wished I could be. Just inside the toilets was this friendly lady with a nice smile.

I plucked up the courage to ask her: "Can I please have a wash and brush up the slate?" expecting to be told to go away.

"Of course you can, me duck," she said. It should have cost two shillings [10p]but I got it for free.

I washed my grubby hands and face then took my stockings off which had loads of ladders in. I rubbed them through with soap and water then put them straight back on. As I emerged from the toilets, my shoes were squelching. I will be forever grateful to that kind toilet attendant.

I would have done anything for Mum's acceptance at this time but each time I went back I could only stay a few days because I felt worthless and suicidal.

So I was homeless yet again and had been walking the streets for well over a week. I was unkempt, my hair was greasy and I was desperate to see Stan. I needed some food because it killed my pain.

I'd spent several days with the down and outs in the city when I bumped into an old school friend.

"Hi, Sylv, how are you?", she asked.

"If you really want to know, I'm homeless," I replied.

She told me where there were some rooms in Alfred Street and I went along to check them out. The place looked grubby on the outside. It was shop-fronted and situated near the pawn shop.

I knocked and waited, then the door opened and what I took to be a Caribbean accent said: "Hello." A huge man stood towering over me. I was a little scared but I was desperate for somewhere to stay.

"I've come for a room," I whispered, "Jenny's sent me."

He asked me in and showed me a dimly lit room with a mattress on the floor and grubby bedclothes. The light bulb was red but I knew that, despite my misgivings, at least this very frightened girl would have a bed.

There was no question of money. Besides, I had none. I told

him I would have the room and as he left I heard the door click. I started to panic. There was no escape and I felt extremely frightened as I lay down on the mattress.

It must have been way past midnight when I awoke [I had left the light on] and heard the door open. I saw shapes and shadows and those eyes, those prying eyes. I knew instantly what was going to happen to me.

That night, I suffered the trauma of being raped three times, I think by three different men. It was difficult to tell how many there were but I was treated like a piece of dirt, something there solely for their pleasure. I couldn't fight them off, they were so strong, and as I lay there being used I wondered what was happening to my life.

How much more of this could I take? Was I, in fact, doing something to encourage men to use me this way? Was I naïve to accept the hospitality of these people and not expect them to want something in return? How I wish today that I had been a little more cynical and mistrusting of people that offered me help because that horrendous experience has stayed with me for the rest of my life.

The rapes seemed to last forever and when I left the building later, I felt I had lost everything ... what had life to offer me now?

I felt worthless. I hated myself and just looking in the mirror caused me so much pain and anger. I could see Dad looking back at me. As I wandered in a state of shock, I wondered whether I had had a nightmare or was all of this really happening?

I remember one time glancing at myself in a shop doorway and seeing my reflection. I looked an absolute wreck. And I felt like one too.

As I wandered up Alfred Street, I felt well and truly broken mentally and in spirit. I didn't want to live. Heaven had to be a better place to be because living on earth had become absolute hell.

Chapter 4

Papplewick perverts

My mind is torn apart by the tiny child inside
Craving for love I have been deprived.
Chips, chocs, crispbread,
Substitutes inside my head.
Self-destructive, I have found,
I feel the need to shout out loud

I hadn't seen Stan for several weeks. He was probably on one of his foreign holidays. But I knew if I saw him I could ease my pain with food, and that's what Stan gave me every time.

I had been sitting on my usual bench in Slab Square for hours in the cold dampness of night, freezing with fear in case anyone dared to speak to me. I hated myself so much that I had been mutilating my arms as I sat there. Then I felt a hand touch me and I jumped with panic. I turned around and saw that it was Stan. At last, he had found me.

"Come on, ducky," he said, "I've got fish and chips and a drink."

I was shivering but relieved when I got into Stan's Morris 1000. I soon got warm and demolished the meal in seconds. I then asked if he had anything else because I wanted to be fat.

Stan interrogated me about what I had been doing. I couldn't tell him what had happened because I knew it was my fault. Why had I been given this body that men seemed to want?

He said he was taking me home but I yelled at him: "No, I want to go to London!" He told me not to be silly and drove to the place we usually ended up, a kind of lovers' hideaway in Papplewick Lane where people went to make love.

I realised that he had bought me my first meal in days and I was grateful for that. But I knew there was always a price to pay. He would want his gratification and he thought that was only fair. After all, he had done me a favour, hadn't he? He had fed me which had helped me to blank out my painful memories, if only for a short time.

As Stan laid me down in the back of the car in Papplewick

AM I NOT A PERSON?

Lane, I chose to shut myself off to what he was doing. But at one stage, when I focused on some movement out of the back window, I realised there was a man pressing his face against the glass. A peeping Tom! Stan was getting his gratification and someone else was getting his kicks from watching us!

Stan leapt up and the pervert ran off through the woods. Stan jumped into the front seat and drove me straight home. He convinced me that being there was better than walking the streets but he didn't know of the cruelty and abuse I would have to endure.

Me at 19 years of age

Inside Aston Hall in the 1960s

Lisa, Mark and Carl at Cleethorpes, June 1976

Chapter 5

Back and forth

Home is where the heart is, everyone says.
But why does Mum act in such a way?

I had managed to get a job as a machinist in a factory. But Mum wasn't content with rejecting me, she now showed that she had totally given up on me. One day, when lunch time came, I eagerly got out my sandwiches but was absolutely horrified to find cold beans on them covered in cigarette ash. It was another way of hurting me.

Of course, I couldn't eat it and I had no money to buy food so once again I was being denied my only solace. Thankfully, Stan met me outside work. He had bought me some new shoes and told me he had found some digs in Sneinton.

To the outsider, Stan was a caring man. To me, he was the provider of food and clothes. I realise now that this was for his own ends but at the time I relished someone lavishing attention on me.

Stan took me to meet a family that was willing to give me a place to stay. When I walked in, I thought it seemed a homely enough place. But the family had one daughter at home who had learning difficulties and after a few weeks I was on the move again due to her feeling pushed out.

But the family seemed to like me and they asked me if I would like to live with their other daughter in Gedling. I agreed to go. This family really put themselves out to help me but my past was taking its toll on my body and mind. I was listless and Elsie, the woman I was living with, decided to fetch the doctor.

He didn't quite know what to make of me and prescribed Librium. Elsie and her husband went to work and I was left on my own in the house. I immediately dug in the cupboards, found some bleach and proceeded to pour it over my private parts. I also started to pull my hair out in chunks. I simply couldn't cope any longer with my mental torture.

This went on for several weeks before Stan called one day,

out of the blue, to see how I was doing. I told him I wanted to go back with him and even though he tried to stop me I flung my case in the back of his car and we set off. I'd left a note thanking Elsie for her wonderful kindness but I simply could not accept it. Now it seemed I couldn't handle it when people were nice to me!

Stan took me back to my Mum's but when we arrived I heard her say dismissively: "Bloody hell, Diana's here." I was angry, really angry and shouted at her: "Why don't you want me!? Why!? What have I done to you?"

Before I knew it, something heavy hit me around the head. It was Danny. He told me not to speak to my mother that way. "Why not?", I asked, starting to sob. "What has she done for me?"

With faultless logic, he yelled at me: "She's your mother!"

I walked out, slamming the door, and went down to my cousin's who lived a few doors away. While I sat talking to her, I wondered just when I was going to feel wanted.

At 9.00pm, I went back home to find the door locked. I knocked and knocked, then eventually Mum opened it, grabbed me, roughly pulled me inside and yelled at me for being out late. I was then sent straight to bed.

I was getting this treatment over and over from Mum and Danny was once again getting his gratification by using me, going through his sickening routine whenever he felt the urge. Clearly, he was getting his kicks by causing me pain mentally and physically. I felt like my body and mind were being continually, violently raped.

I simply couldn't cope. I knew I had to escape. I knew that if I didn't tell someone I would end up in the River Trent, just another suicide statistic.

Yet again, I packed my case and walked out of Mum's. At times I wished I could see Stan and then at other times I hated him so much because he was using me for his own pleasure just like all the others. So this time, I dumped my suitcase at a holding place at Huntingdon Street bus station. I had decided that I was going to escape and that I would speak out.

I hopped on a Trent bus and what little money I had bought a single ticket to Buxton in Derbyshire. When the bus pulled out of the inner city and I saw the open fields I felt free ... free from everyone.

AM I NOT A PERSON?

I arrived in Buxton bewildered, hungry and very cold. It was winter, night began to fall very early, and even at 16 I really couldn't handle the dark. What if I somebody grabbed me, what if I was raped, what if ...

I was starting to get very scared. After walking for what seemed an age, I saw a police station in the distance. I walked in and went to the desk.

"Hello, love."

The police officer seemed a caring soul. His voice was reassuring. I wanted to blurt everything out, everything that had happened. About my Dad, about Danny and his disgusting acts, about Stan and everybody else who had abused me ... mentally, physically. But those eyes haunted me, stopping me from saying what I wanted to say.

As if the sound was coming from somewhere else, I heard myself utter the words: "I've been dumped."

"Come in here, love," said the policeman and took me into a warm room. He asked another officer to make me a hot drink. "What's happened then, lovey?"

I said: "Well, a man picked me up and his hands were everywhere."

In reality I was talking about the house of horrors but didn't dare for the life of me name any of the real abusers. I started to cry and a supporting arm went around my shoulders.

"There's a twinkle in her eye," said the officer, "that shows she is telling the truth."

I *was* telling the truth. My body had been touched from my earliest memory. I wanted so desperately to break the chains wrapped around me. But it never happened. I was put into a police car and once again taken back to Mum's. I felt like a yo-yo ... back and forth, back and forth.

I stuck it at Mum's for a day or so until I went to my cousin's and she told me about some lodgings in Regent Street. Somebody had mentioned these in the past but I had been too scared to take the first step. I felt and looked like a worthless, lost soul and the memory of what happened last time I sought out some digs was still extremely vivid.

Stan had disappeared yet again and I was worried because he was the provider of the only comfort I had. Then, one day he contacted me and arranged to meet in Carlton Road on one of my visits to my Aunt's. But he didn't show up and I made my own way into Nottingham city centre, determined to find somewhere to live. The Girls Friendly Society hostel was situated where all the private dentists' and doctors' surgeries were, in a 'posh' part of Nottingham. I found the hostel and made my way to the front door, put down my case and rang the bell. A few seconds later, a nice-looking lady opened the door.

"Can I help you?" she enquired. She was quite tall and very 'old-fashioned'.

"Yes," I said in a weak voice. "I heard you let rooms off for girls."

"That's right," she said, "would you like to come in?"

I dropped my case on the floor [my hand was throbbing] while she took a few details. I hoped I would be able to stay. While she asked me questions I struggled to block out any thoughts of my house of horrors.

She took my name then asked me why I was homeless.

Without hesitation I said: "My Mum's dead and the rest of my family live in Australia."

"Oh dear, lovey," she said, "I'm sure we can help you."

I wished in my heart that my Mum really was dead. She had caused me so much pain in my life and I desperately wanted to rid myself of it. While I sat there, I thought that the probation officer, Mrs Barton, was bound to be looking for me. I had already missed several appointments with her.

The warden showed me around and I felt a warmth I had not felt for years. I was shown my room on the top floor, with fitted carpets and lovely divan beds. £3 and 5 shillings [£3.25] a week and you had to put shillings in the meter for gas.

The warden told me I was to share with a girl called Jill, who would be in shortly. She had been brought up in Dr Barnardo's homes and when I met her I warmed instantly to her lovely personality. We were to share the bathroom and I was told that if I used it, I cleaned it.

"Oh, yes," I said enthusiastically.

I tried to think of this as my new start and I was happy there for a while. Stan eventually found out where I was [he made a habit of tracking me down] and I was grateful when he paid for the cost of my digs … but once again, I found out that this generosity had a price and that he expected me to provide him with sexual favours. He provided me with food and paid for the roof over my head. Was it right for him to demand sex in return?

But even though I liked my new place, the flashbacks were there every waking hour. The screams of my rape were there to shudder through my body. There was simply no escape.

It got so bad that I started to dread waking up because I would see my reflection in the mirror once more. I hated the sight of it so much, of my father's features staring back at me, that I clawed and clawed at my face until it bled.

Jill saw my injuries and couldn't understand why I had done such a thing. But she didn't know of my inner torment and pain. Nevertheless, she didn't criticise me. In fact, she tried to talk to me.

I also started to eat soap powder around this time because I wanted to cleanse the filth in my body. I was being destroyed, it was like a cancer eating away at my mind. I felt like I just couldn't take any more.

One night, I put on a pretty satin night-dress, put a cushion under my head near the gas fire, turned it on and just laid there. I had filled up the meter with all the shillings I had. I wanted to end my nightmare.

The next thing I remember was waking up in Nottingham General Hospital. I had been in hospital about a day when the warden from my digs arrived to see me.

"Hi, Sylvia, how are you?"

"Why was I found?!" I said.

"Don't be silly," she said in a very cross voice, "you have everything to live for."

There was a deathly silence before she added quietly: "Look Sylvia, I want to talk to you about your mother."

My heart started to race.

"Well," she continued, "she knocked on my door today and asked for you. When I told her she couldn't be your mother because your mother had died, she said she was very much alive."

The warden was clearly in a state of shock. She just couldn't understand why I had told her my Mum was dead. But it was obvious to me. She had neglected me from as long ago as I can remember and this was the best way to block out my pain. It would have been easier for me to accept that she was dead rather than face her rejection just one more time.

AM I NOT A PERSON?

I was told that I couldn't go back to the Girls Friendly Society so, once again, Mrs Barton took me back to my Mum's house.

Chapter 6

Seventeen and unloved

Doesn't anyone care?
They only stop and stare.
The tear-stained face,
The face of sadness,
The face of rejection.
When will someone rescue this inner child?

My life had been sheer hell the 17 years that I had been on the earth. Even Mrs Barton was taking Mum's side. Why didn't she realise what I was going through? It is clear to me now that my behaviour then was classic of an abused child, yet nobody recognised it.

I felt unloved. Worthless. All the time I was at home it was torture. The times I was left alone I would just lay on my grubby bedclothes and sob my heart out. I needed Mum so much. I wanted her to love me but why did she hate me? The cruelty never stopped, day in, day out. Sheer, mental torture.

Over a period of a year or more, Mum had regularly contacted the police for help with how to deal with me. They advised her to take a court order out and so she contacted the social services.

One day, after I had been home for some weeks, I got up as usual to go to work [I'd found another job] but Mum told me not to bother because somebody was coming to see me. I knew it was certainly an important visitor because Mum had taken the trouble to tidy around.

It didn't take much to guess who it was because no-one had shown an interest in me for 16 years ... only men and for all the wrong reasons.

It would be Mrs Barton, the probation officer. By now I hadn't seen her in months and I figured that Mum had probably contacted her. Apparently, Mum told the department that I had been running away from home and staying out late. She also told them I had tried to take my life, all of which was true. But didn't anybody ever ask why?

AM I NOT A PERSON?

Whenever I went to Mrs Barton's office, she would just ask me continually what job I wanted to do. It seems that if you had a work ethic there was nothing wrong with you. I remember somebody even suggested that I was a no-hoper interested only in living off the National Assistance. What an insult!

On one occasion, Mrs Barton took me to the careers office to try to get me a job as a nurse in the Navy. I wasn't accepted. Obviously, I was very unkempt and first impressions must have put them off. Also, I had no qualifications, which was a major factor in itself.

Sometimes when I went to see Mrs Barton I would just sit there in a trance, the eyes of my abusers haunting me all the time. Why did the so-called caring professions not pick up on what was really affecting my behaviour?

The reason Mrs Barton was visiting is that before she could arrange a court hearing, she had to see me to write a report. When she arrived, Mum put the kettle on.

"Well, Sylvia," said Mrs Barton, "how are you?"

"All right," I whispered.

"You're doing well at your job aren't you?" Yet again, work was a primary concern.

I looked at her with contempt. I wanted to tell her about the horrors I was experiencing but all I said was: "I like my job."

"Well," she went on, "your Mum's been having problems with you."

I stared at her in disbelief: "What problems?!"I said, looking from her to Mum and back again.

"Staying out late, back-chatting ..."

I wanted to tell her so much but I didn't dare. The abuse from Neville and Danny was destroying me. And to make it worse, as I sat there with Mrs Barton, one of my abusers came into the room to warm himself. I just clammed up.

Then Mrs Barton and Mum went into the front parlour to discuss what the next move was. Neville had disappeared to tinker with his cars. When Mrs Barton had left, I was made to wash up the greasy pots in cold water. Then Mum told me that I was to go to court.

I was petrified but I managed to arrange to meet Stan and tell him what was going on. He provided me with a lovely, yummy steak pie and chips. While I bolted it down, I repeatedly asked Stan what it all meant and why was I going to court.

AM I NOT A PERSON?

Within two weeks, the court date had arrived and I was taken in, sandwiched between Mrs Barton and Mum. There were no words of comfort from Mum. An usher appeared, dressed in his black gown, and finalised a few points with Mrs Barton. I began to shake.

Then I was led into the courthouse. I was scared. Scared of the unknown. What had I done to be here in front of this court? There was a row of people I'd never seen before who were going to decide my fate. I just stood there, twisting my hanky around and around, not believing that this was happening.

Mrs Barton came over and told me not to worry and to speak clear and loud. Mum had disappeared to sit and listen to the proceedings. The huge wooden benches dwarfed me.

"What am I doing here?" I kept asking myself. I was only 17.

I was told to stand and the judge read out that I was "beyond parental control". Then I looked across and caught the eye of one of my abusers. The look he gave me as he read the oath out loud sent shivers through my body.

The judge questioned him about my worsening behaviour. As he told his story, I stood and faced this monster and started to sob uncontrollably. I was so, so scared. My life had been hell and here I was before the courts through no fault of my own.

I felt at this moment that Mrs Barton had failed me miserably.

I knew that I should have been taking the oath so that I could spill the beans. I was screaming inside. I knew that the right place for this man telling "the truth, the whole truth and nothing but the truth" was prison with the key thrown away.

Neville told lie after lie. Was he so scared of me speaking out? I knew this was his way of silencing me. Everything was moving so fast as Neville sealed my fate. Everybody was talking about me but not to me. Once again, my voice went unheard.

I wiped my face and was asked once again to stand. I tried to look at the judge, hoping he would get me out of this nightmare. I hoped he would see through Neville's lies and realise I was a normal teenager. I hoped he would recognise that I was going through hell.

As I stared at him he said: "Now then, Sylvia, would you like to go somewhere with a swimming pool and nice grounds?"

I thought he was about to send me on a wonderful holiday. It sounded just like paradise, maybe just what I had been looking for.

AM I NOT A PERSON?

"Yes," I said as the tears began to flow again. The ordeal was proving too much for me and Mrs Barton gave me another hanky.

I was scared and angry. I wanted Neville to be charged with the crimes he had committed on me. I wanted to take the oath because I knew that if I spoke out in the courthouse the police would protect me ... wouldn't they?

Chapter 7

The forgotten people

A lost identity in Aston Hall,
Locked away through no fault of my own.
Juvenile delinquents, that's what they say,
Cart them off and throw away the key.
No-one to listen to our cries of shame.
No-one to listen to our pain.

So they assigned me to Aston Hall for assessment. Mum left me in court without a word of goodbye and Neville had succeeded in silencing me ... not for the first time in my life.

When I left the courts and sat in the car squashed between two police officers, I knew there was no escape. I was a bewildered, disoriented teenager. As the car sped on its way I realised from the road signs that we were heading for Derby. There was an eerie silence, not a word spoken, and I was soon to find out why.

Before long, I saw in the distance a huge building with areas of land and several buildings surrounding it. I was later to find out that these were wards accommodating so-called misfits in society.

But it wasn't their fault. They were housed in these wards because society could not accept them. My cousin was a resident of one of these wards and I can still hear her piercing screams. The only crime she had committed was having two children out of wedlock.

The car went up the drive and came to a sudden halt. My arm was grabbed and I was led to a door which was opened by a nurse with a huge key around her neck. When I walked inside, she immediately locked the door behind her. As I waited, the officer told the nurse that I had come straight from the juveniles court. They knew I would be arriving ... they had prepared the clinic room.

I was left in the corridor and waited, as I was told to. I was very scared. Then a nurse beckoned me to the clinic room where she told me to get undressed. Once again, I was being

45

stripped of any dignity that I had, being made to undress in front of strangers and having a man touch me.

As I laid on the bed, an elderly man examined my chest, heaven knows why. Then he looked at my nails.

"Oh, you are a naughty girl," he said, "biting your nails."

Was there any wonder?

He then made me lie down to do something to me down below. I think he used a swab but I couldn't be sure. After I was weighed he told me to follow the nurse and my head was checked for lice.

I was then led to the store cupboard to be given my regulation clothing, a checked dress in material that made my skin itch. I felt as if I was wearing a scouring pad. My vest and knickers were labelled and I was given regulation socks. Then my hair was cut. It looked as if they'd used a basin.

Next, they led me into the dining area where lunch was being served. I glanced around the hall and saw that everyone was dressed the same and all had identical haircuts. Regulation.

All the horrible memories of school suddenly came flooding back. Why was this happening to me? I just couldn't understand why I had been brought to Aston.

I vividly remember being assessed. I would be given simple little tasks which I sometimes couldn't do because my mind was in turmoil.

I was assigned to a girls' ward called Laburnum. There was a boys' ward opposite called Beech. Clearly, they had decided I was verging on the sub-normal because the only task they reckoned I could do was weaving.

Every morning we would be woken up in the dormitory, given breakfast, then escorted to school. I just used to sit in a chair wondering when I would be rescued. I blamed Neville and I blamed Mum. My arms were reaching out but she wasn't there. As I sat in my chair I started to cry. My heart was breaking. I needed Mum, I needed Stan, I needed a soul mate. But who could I confide in at Aston, with the ward run under such a strict regime?

The beds in the dormitory were made of cast iron and the bathroom was communal. There were two baths inside and the staff made us line up naked in the corridor to have our baths. Then the nursing staff washed us. Wasn't this just another form of abuse?

AM I NOT A PERSON?

There was a side room next to the dorm which was used by the doctor when he gave the 'truth drug' to young girls. He would soak some gauze in ether and before long the girls were screaming. I heard this awful sound so many times and my mind began to race, wondering just what was happening to these girls while under the influence of the ether.

As the days turned into weeks, I started to pick up the routine. After breakfast and school, our letters were given to us and we were allowed to write once a month. Meal times involved everyone sitting down together. At the front of the dining hall was a long serving table and anyone classed as difficult would be placed at the end.

There was a girl called Mavis who was heavily pregnant. She was a pretty girl with red hair and freckles. She was on the long table and was being force fed. I felt so sorry for her that I began to cry, for which I was punished by having to scrub the stairs for hours. I had only shown genuine emotions.

I was also put into the side room for answering back to a member of staff. For five days I stayed in a cold, harsh room with a bare mattress on the floor. I was only let out for 10 minutes at a time to slop my waste bucket out. My friends helped to keep me sane by slipping comics under the door.

One of the friends I made at Aston was Jane. Despite our sadness, we often had a laugh together. One afternoon, we sat writing our letters when Jane's name was called. She was to have the 'truth treatment'.

"Sylv," she said, "what am I going to do? I'm scared."

She had heard the other girls screaming. My arm went around her shoulder, I told her not to worry and that I would be there for her. She started to shake and cry but I told her to stop because showing normal emotions was a crime.

A while later, many of us were taken to another ward called Mansion, where it seemed people had been incarcerated for over 20 years. You could see your reflection like a mirror image on the floor and there was an overpowering aroma of lavender polish. They gave us a sewing lesson then escorted us back to the other ward.

When I walked in, the smell of ether hit me. Jane! I wanted to see her so desperately. On my way to the toilet I managed to glance through the window of the side room and saw her unconscious. As I walked back down the stairs it struck me that we were all being abused here ... this time by the system.

By now, I had been in Aston Hall for well over a month and it was like hell on earth. I longed to be rescued but even though Stan visited me once, there seemed little hope of getting out.

One foggy morning, we were being escorted to school when I saw another group of patients from the long-term ward being taken to the laundry to work. As the group got closer I heard a voice: "Sylvia, Sylvia."

When I turned around there was my cousin. Although she had been in Aston a few years, she hadn't forgotten me. She asked me how I was but she looked a little jaded herself.

Within seconds we were moved on but I couldn't stop thinking about her. Many is the time I glanced out of the window and saw her group being moved about the facility.

Like the letters, you were allowed a visit once a month and on one occasion I was pleased to see my local vicar. He had not forgotten me.

He told me he was trying to get permission for me to have an afternoon out with him and his family. He wrote to the hospital with this request, also adding that he would be able to find me a loving home with a Christian family. Sadly, his offer was rebuffed by the authorities.

It used to break my heart whenever we were taken to the so-called low grade wards. Most of the people there had communication problems and a lot of them were in wheel-chairs.

Some were unable to feed themselves. Around their necks were rubber bibs which chafed on their chins, making them red raw. They were just left there, dribbling, their mouths and runny noses left unattended. I used to call them the forgotten people. How could the human race be so cruel? There was no form of stimulation for their bodies or minds.

In recent years, I have returned to Aston Hall and I am glad to report that things have improved. Patients are no longer stripped of their dignity and they have stimulating environments to help them. But there is still room for further improvement].

After precisely 155 days, I finally got my release from hell. When Mrs Barton gave me my release date, she told me that if I was brought before the courts again I could find myself back in

AM I NOT A PERSON?

Aston Hall. On the day Mrs Barton arrived to collect me, she had a painted smile on her face and said gleefully: "How are you?"

All I felt was immense anger towards her. She had helped me to be incarcerated in Aston Hall! But I didn't tell her my real feelings because it might jeopardise my release. I just told her that I was well and I couldn't wait to get out.

Recently, I gained access to a document relating to my referral to Aston Hall [described as "a place of safety"] which was written for the Clerk to the Justices, Nottingham Juvenile Court.

The report stated that I was prone to running away from difficulties. It added that I exhibited "childish, dependent, apathetic behaviour" and that I could not hold down a job, in fact I was described as "virtually unemployable". The report also stated that an IQ test carried out on me showed my intelligence to be not much above sub-normality.

It added that the way I slouched in my chair and was withdrawn would make it hard for me to live in the community. I was a disturbed, unhappy girl with a low personal valuation.

Well, they got that bit right!

But it wasn't all one-sided. The report did recognise that my mother was "a peculiar woman with a somewhat refined air, but both she and her home are rather unkempt". It said she was a "somewhat neurotic woman who remains constantly with her deceased husband in mind and spirit".

The report also stated that my Mum had complained of my "dirty habits". It makes me so angry to see all too clearly that she was trying to get me locked away for life.

They identified that maternal rejection was probably an important causative factor in my behaviour but there were indications of other emotional problems.

It stated that while they could not entirely discount that I was experiencing a more serious psychological breakdown often seen in adolescence, there was no positive evidence of this.

The probation officer's report said: "Although on present evidence I could not recommend compulsory action under the Mental Health Act, I think she is in need of a period of hospital care and treatment."

Two years later, this information was used to seal my fate yet again. After another of my suicide attempts, a letter was sent to Mapperley Hospital from my probation officer.

Accompanied by the Aston report, the letter asked for me to be seen by a psychiatrist, adding that I had already been seen by a doctor at the General Hospital.

The letter said that I had been drifting around aimlessly in a very confused state of mind. It seems I wanted to leave Nottingham but had no idea where I wanted to go.

The report back from the doctor at Mapperley to my probation officer described me as an "aimless, feckless person who reacts to everything with a feeling of being fed up". It made out that I did not like anybody or anything ... my family, my job, my lodgings, that I had no aim in life and that I seemed unable to form lasting human relationships.

How could anybody write such damning reports about me? This label has followed me right through my adult life and has made me extremely angry. The hospital had failed to recognise the signs of abuse and decided to leave me to my own devices.

Chapter 8

Freedom?

Walking along the lined Chase
The rain splashing on my face.
The earthy smells rising from the ground,
Nature's wonderful, I have found.
The spiders spinning their webs,
Dew glistening like diamonds on display.
Nobody can take Nature's wonderment away.
I sit in the park, in my garden of freedom.
The snow is falling, twisting and whirling, shining like jewels.
The robins, the sparrows, fighting for food,
As I sit and forget my pain for a while.

As we left Aston Hall, Mrs Barton told me that she had found me a residential job ... as a nanny to a severely disabled child. I suppose part of me was pleased, but my life was no longer my own. How dare they find jobs for me without even asking?

She told me as we got into the car that the job was in Sherwood, north Nottingham, and I was initially horrified when I found out what my new job entailed. I had to get Henry up, dress him, and see that he was picked up to take him to and from his special needs school.

Henry couldn't communicate. He just sat there, rocking. I felt an enormous amount of pity for him and I gave him all my devotion and love. I tried so very hard to help him with his communication skills but I also gave him lots of hugs and kisses. I knew when he was happy because he would shake and give me a huge smile.

But not only did I feel that I had been dumped at this house, I also found the job very demanding. After all, I was only a teenager. I was almost on the point of exhaustion and I was desperate to see Stan. I wanted him to know that I was out of Aston.

On my day off, I travelled to my dear Aunt Meg's. She showed me in and there was Stan, sitting on the sofa. He gave me the usual nod and I knew that he would meet me shortly on

AM I NOT A PERSON?

London Road. Not long after, Stan left Aunty's and I followed 10 minutes later. I ran to his car and started to cry.

I told him that I hated it in Sherwood. Henry's mum had shouted at me for giving him too much attention and I was confused. How could anyone tell me off for caring too much?

Later that day I went into Mrs Barton's office and told her that I hated my job. I had to keep going to see her, it was one of the conditions of my release. She seemed to understand and assured me that she would find me another residential job.

Some days later, Mrs B came to tell me she had found the ideal job for me. I had already served my notice at Sherwood and was not sorry to go, although I was sad at leaving Henry. The new job was in West Bridgford, referred to by Nottingham people at the time as 'bread and lard island'.

I was to be a residential cook and housekeeper to a very successful couple who had a mansion set in acres of land. After the introductions, I was shown into my room. It was good to be around a family again, but I still felt alone. The family had bought me a nice suit with a lovely hat but that didn't compensate for my emptiness.

I was left on my own for long periods when I was expected to cook and clean the house. Most of the time, I would be eating out of their pantry. By now, my compulsion with food was taking over my life. I had gone into Aston Hall in December 1964 weighing 149lbs and had come out in April 1965 tipping the scales at 161lbs.

On my days off, I would dress up to meet Stan but on my way there I would get wolf whistles from the men who were working nearby. I knew I was attractive but I felt so scared.

One day, when the family was out, Stan popped in. "How are you, ducky?" he said, to which I replied: "I hate it, Stan, I'm lonely."

I explained how, once I had served the meals to the family, I had to sit in the kitchen eating my meal on my own. I showed him around the house, with its cabinets full of silver which I had to polish. I also showed him my room, which was nicely furnished, then another which had boxes and boxes of chocolates stacked high. Just then, he heard a car and said he'd better go.

My eating was now out of control, but it anaesthetised my emotions. The rejection I felt when sent to the kitchen to eat my meals was hurting me. And the stack of chocolates was haunting me. I had to have some.

Not long after, when I was alone again in the house, I walked into the area where the chocolates were kept and took some. I felt like a child again, frightened of being shouted at. I walked into the loo and hastily ate the chocolate, flushing the paper down the toilet so that I wouldn't be found out. But it wasn't long before I was hauled in front of my employers.

"Sylvia," they said, "we only take on staff who are honest and trustworthy." I knew what was going to happen. "There is a bar of chocolate missing. Have you had it?"

"No," I said, yet I could feel my colour rising. They asked me again if I had taken it and again I said "No".

There was silence for a second or two and I felt ashamed of myself. Not only for taking the chocolate but for lying too.

"Well Sylvia," they continued, "why was the chocolate wrapping down the toilet?"

I couldn't argue with them. I felt disgust for myself for what I did and for losing their trust. From then on, I wasn't trusted an inch and the job became unbearable.

I had arranged to meet Stan again on my day off and he was there, as usual. He had bought me the biggest jacket potato, covered in with thick, creamy coleslaw and I was soon stuffing my face. My arms were in overdrive getting the food to my mouth and my pain disappeared for a while.

Stan kept telling me to take my time and not to cram food into my face so fast. But I was filling an emptiness. When I'd finished eating, I told Stan that I was leaving West Bridgford.

"You can't, duck," he said, "you might land back in Aston Hall."

"Can't I?" I said.

That bit of fire that was left in me made sure that I did move out. They treated me as a nobody and I left without a goodbye. I met Stan with my suitcase and felt as free as a bird. I was even willing to face homelessness again. Then Stan told me about some lodgings on Pym Street, but I said I had no money.

"I'll pay the bill for you," he said, "just go and see the old dear. She won't charge a lot. She lives on her own."

He went on to say that he thought I would be good for her and she would be good for me.

He took me over to see her in her three-storey terrace near to

AM I NOT A PERSON?

St Ann's Well Road. I pulled my suitcase out of Stan's car and made my way to the door. A small, smartly dressed woman greeted me and asked me in. I put my case in her front room and she showed me her dining room which had a coal fire burning.

"Would you like a cuppa, duck?" she said, and I readily accepted.

She told me she would charge me £3 all-in then asked me my likes and dislikes. We had a good old natter, then she showed me my new room. As I went up the stairs I noticed that the house was spotless. There was a kidney-shaped walnut dresser in the bedroom with three mirrors on it and the bedclothes looked brand new. When we came back downstairs she asked me what I thought.

"It's lovely," I said, "when can I move in?"

"Now, if you like," she said, and before she could change her mind I gave her a week's board in advance.

As I started to unpack she came upstairs to see me. She didn't ask about my past because I think Stan had filled her in with some kind of story. Instead, she just walked into the room and handed me a huge bottle of Topaz perfume.

"Here love," she said, "put this on your dresser."

This dear old soul made me feel wanted. She used to make my favourite meal for me on a Friday ... tripe and onions and mashed potatoes. I remember in one of our many chats when she told me: "You have to look after number one in this world. Nobody else will do it for you."

Her words rang true. For the first time ever, I felt like I mattered. I called her Mue. She was the mother figure I had been waiting for. She even warmed my slippers for me and gave me the respect I felt I deserved. Even though I continued to have the horrific flashbacks, I appreciated how kind she was to me.

She would buy me tights and do little things that will live with me forever. She even took the trouble to put a hot water bottle in my bed for me. I had never known such luxuries.

I had been at Mue's for well over six months and I had been meeting Stan on a regular basis. He was pleased that I was a little happier and continued to buy me clothes and any food that I wanted. By now, I had moved on to chocolates and crisps but my body was still attractive. I hated it.

AM I NOT A PERSON?

Summer was fast approaching and Stan informed me he had booked a four berth caravan in Caister-on-Sea near Great Yarmouth. I was 18 years old and about to experience my first real holiday. I was really excited but this was tempered by another emotion. As I packed my bags, I knew there would be a price to pay ... Stan would want his sexual gratification once more.

Mue waved me off and we drove down the street in the blazing sun. I had never known a summer so hot. While I was at the caravan I caught the sun and ended up looking like a lobster. Calamine lotion did nothing to ease my agony! But I enjoyed the social side of the holiday and I didn't want it to end.

The only good thing about going back was that I was pleased to see Mue and she seemed pleased to see me. As we walked into the dining room, where she had laid out a lovely salad, I handed her a little present that I'd picked up at the coast.

Shortly after my holidays I began to feel unwell and was sick on a regular basis. But I continued doing my work, once again as a machinist. It was the longest time I had held a job down.

My sickness continued but worse was to follow. I had missed a period. Now I was scared. I daren't for the life of me tell Mue ... she might reject me. I was also worried that if Mrs Barton found out she might send me back to Aston Hall. Yet again, my mind was in a mess, but I had to tell somebody.

I arranged to meet Stan and as soon as he pulled up in his car I blurted out: "I'm pregnant."

For a moment there was silence, broken only by: "Pregnant, Sylv?" from Stan. He said it as if he had no idea what I was talking about.

"What am I going to do, Stan?" I said. "I can't tell Mue."

"Don't you worry, ducky," he said, as if there wasn't a problem, but it was easy for him. I stood to lose much more. For the first time in years I was happy. No abuse by the monsters, just genuine caring and love from Mue. I knew that Stan was abusing me in another way, but I had a pleasant home environment for the first time ever.

But again, my happiness was not to last. I had gone to work as usual one day and on my arrival home I was told by one of Mue's neighbours that she had been rushed into hospital.

I knew she had no family and I instantly made my way to the

Nottingham General Hospital, only to be told that Mue had died in the ambulance.

I was heartbroken. I hadn't known her for long, but I knew in my heart that she was an angel.

After Mue died, I was informed by her landlord that I had two weeks after the funeral to vacate the premises.

The neighbours organised her funeral and I did my best to sort her belongings out. She had a comfortable home and she cared about other people so I organised the furnishings to go to the Family First trust.

As I packed to leave Pym Street, I carefully wrapped the Topaz perfume Mue had given me. I shut Mue's door for the last time and felt angry that I had to leave this house which had so many happy memories. Stan didn't have a clue what had happened. He was working away.

Chapter 9

Homeless and pregnant

It took many years to speak out the truth
And let the world know how I lost my youth.

Once again I was homeless, only this time I was pregnant. And again, I began to be absent from work. My mind was in turmoil; the person who had given me guidance had left me for a better place and I'd had to vacate her house.

I was desperate to see Stan. I had no income and I wondered where I was going to end up. I knew I would never go home. Again, I had not seen Mrs Barton for months and I was pleased.

I made my way to Aunty Meg's in the Meadows but she had a full house so I knew I couldn't stay there. As I wandered to town, Stan pulled up in his car with his uncanny knack of finding me. He asked me why I had left Mue's.

"She's dead!" I screamed and started to cry again. He took me to Trent Bridge and laid a blanket on the steps so we could sit and talk. Then he told me he had been talking to friends and they had advised him to give me Quinine, gin and whisky to abort my unborn child. He had the concoction with him and offered it to me.

"I'm not taking that!" I yelled.

"Come on!" he screamed back and tried to get me to take it. In the end, as his anger raged out of control, he threw the mixture into the River Trent. I knew he was cross with me but I wanted this gift of life, to give it my love and everything I had been denied.

A few weeks later, I wandered aimlessly into town on one of my long walks in the night. I felt so hungry and was wondering where I could find food when I looked up and saw that I was passing Browns Bakery on Arkwright Street. There was a bin liner outside. I peered in and saw that for the first time in 24 hours I would be able to feed my unborn child. I crammed the contents of the bag into my mouth as fast as I could. These sweet cakes and savoury pastries were destined for the pig bins but they had taken my hunger away for a while. After I had had my fill, I slowly continued on to town.

I was angry with the plight I was in. Stan was the man who should provide for me but he was married and living the life of Riley. When I arrived in the city centre I sat in my usual place in Slab Square watching the world go by and visualising what life could be like if Stan committed himself to me. I hadn't seen him for a few weeks but, as before, he suddenly appeared in his car. I was both happy and angry to see him.

"Where have you been?!" I shouted.

"I've been to Spain, Sylv," he said matter-of-factly. "Are you all right, ducky?"

"I'm just a sex object for you, Stan," I yelled at him. "You don't care about me do you? I've been walking for days now while you have been living it up. You don't care that I'm having your baby, do you?"

It was the first time I had opened up and shown him how angry I was. We walked to his car and there wasn't a word said, then I just sat there staring into the distance.

"Here you are, duck," Stan said and presented me with my favourite treat; an elephant's foot, a huge pastry full of cream and covered in chocolate.

Despite my recent 'feast', I crammed the pastry in my mouth as if it was the only food I'd seen in weeks.

"Haven't you had anything to eat?" Stan asked, amazed at the speed the cake was being devoured.

"Yes," I blurted out between bites. "Out of a pig bag."

Looking totally confused, he started the car and told me he wanted to talk to me. He drove to Papplewick Lane again and parked up. Then he told me plainly that he didn't want naming over the baby. He convinced me it was vital that nobody knew he was the father.

Of course, after this little chat he got his gratification again. Why else would he have taken me to Papplewick Lane? He'd figured that once he had satisfied my urge he would be able to satisfy his own. And I let him. I knew I was being used but I just couldn't do anything about it. He helped to anaesthetise my pain, my anger and my emptiness.

I felt so cheap and started to sob as we drove back. I said: "Why should I save your face, Stan? I'm having your child!" Then I repeated: "Do you care about me or your baby?"

AM I NOT A PERSON?

Without waiting for an answer I added: "Drop me off at Aunty's," and he did just that. Then he disappeared again to his cosy marriage and his cosy house.

As I walked into Aunty's place I saw she was alone, busy tidying her small lounge. I sat down and blurted out that I was pregnant.

"Who's the dad?" she immediately asked.

I desperately wanted to tell her Stan was, but he had warned me against it.

"It's somebody in Mansfield," I said.

"Does your mum know?"

"No, I don't want to tell her."

Mum hadn't wanted me all of my life and I was sure she wouldn't want me now.

I told Aunty I had nowhere to live. I hadn't had any proper rest for days and I started to feel so weak and ill. So I left Aunty's, went to Slab Square, and stretched out and catnapped for an hour or so.

I was about four months into my pregnancy and my stomach had started to swell. I was happy that I was getting fatter because the threat of any man looking at me was diminishing. I had been homeless for weeks now and would spend most nights walking into Nottingham along Queens Drive, which was renowned for prostitutes and kerb crawlers. It was about 11.30pm when I heard footsteps behind me. I was petrified and walked near the road to let whoever it was pass me. Then I heard a man's voice.

"What's a nice girl like you doing out this time of night?"

I froze.

"Look, duck," the voice went on, "you are in so much danger walking up here. Come to my place for a coffee."

"No, no, I'm going," I spluttered, but he got hold of my arm.

"I have recently lost my wife," he said. "Come and have a coffee."

I eventually agreed and went with him. He lived in an upstairs flat and even as we approached I looked for an escape route. But I was so hungry and thirsty and I hadn't seen Stan in days. Had he deserted me?

I walked into the flat and it seemed like a mansion. The man made me a cup of coffee using milk then showed me pictures of his wife and started to shed a tear. Here I was in a total stranger's home trying to comfort him. I was trying to ease this man's grief and kept telling him his wife was beautiful. He showed me her wardrobe which was full of her clothes. The dressing table was covered in feminine creams and perfumes. It was a little bit eerie but he seemed a kind man. He eventually asked me my name.

"Sylv," I replied.

"Right, you sleep in here and I will sleep in the lounge."

I was grateful for this man's generosity but on the other hand I was petrified that he still might rape me. I didn't sleep at all. But this man was the first male in my life not interested in abusing me. The next morning he gave me coffee and toast, thanked me for listening and told me to look after myself.

I was on my way again, where I didn't know, but I wandered to my usual haunts in Nottingham. As I sat in Slab Square, I realised the flashbacks, the worthlessness, my whole situation was taking its toll on my body and mind. I wanted to die. I was also pregnant and desperate for the father to make a commitment to me. But he was living his cosy life while I was homeless. It had been four days since I'd seen Stan.

I was so hungry and as I wandered back to my Aunt's to see if I could cadge a cuppa, I bumped into an old school chum. We got talking and she told me she was leaving Nottingham to go to London.

"Are you coming Sylv?" she asked, just like that. "I will pay your fare."

I knew anything was better than the way I was living in Nottingham, so I arranged to meet her before 5.00pm, not really knowing what was ahead of me. As I slowly walked down Queens Drive to Aunty's, who should appear again but Stan. He pulled up and I got into his car.

"I'm going to London, Stan," I said. "On the 5 o'clock train."

He didn't utter a word as he set off but what he did was make damn sure I didn't arrive at the Midlands Station on time. When he finally got me there, my friend had gone, so Stan took me back to the car and asked if I wanted dropping off at Meg's. "Buy me something to eat first," I told him, annoyed that I'd missed the train, so he drove to a shop and bought me several bags of crisps. Then, once again, he dumped me at Aunty's.

She dished me up a bowl of corned beef stew which I demolished then set off again on my wanders, unkempt and very, very disillusioned. This pattern repeated itself day in, day out. I remember one time, as I walked towards the city centre, I started to feel ill and found myself swaying. I felt faint and sat on the pavement. A police officer came over and asked me if I was all right. I wished I was. Homeless and pregnant was not an ideal situation to be in but I told him I would be fine. It was probably my baby turning, but part of me wanted to go to the police station because I would at least have a bed for the night.

The policeman left and I busied myself window shopping. This babe was going to have everything I had been denied, I told myself as I gazed at the goods in the shops. Then I heard a car beep its horn. Yet again, Stan had found me. I'd only just climbed into his car when he told me that I needed a bath.

"Tell me about it!" I said, almost screaming the words.

I was so angry. It was his fault just as much as mine that I was pregnant. I needed him so badly but all he did was hand me the cost of a bath and towel and drop me off at the public baths. I was hurt and I knew he was controlling me.

After my bath, Stan took me to Papplewick again to get his sexual gratification. Was that why he'd paid for me to get cleaned up? I knew I was being abused again but Stan constantly told me that he loved me. But how could I be in this plight if he really loved me?

After Stan had got his kicks and was driving back towards town, I told him to let me out. I was livid. He pulled up at some traffic lights and I jumped out of the car. I walked for a while, as usual making my way to Queens Drive, but when I got to the bottom of the road Stan was there. He'd known where I was going and had waited.

He ordered me into the car but I screamed at him: "No!" and started to cry.

At this moment I hated him so much. I tried to run off but lost my shoe. Stan grabbed me and pushed me into the car. Then he drove to the police station and asked for assistance. I was taken inside where Stan spun his yarn.

"Look, officer," he said, "I have brought Sylvia here because I feel she is in mortal danger."

I was horrified. This man who was supposed to love me was handing me over to the police. My bags were searched and I was taken into a room with a policewoman. While I sat there bewildered and angry at Stan, I was asked questions, during which I blurted out: "I'm pregnant!"

The police officer was so kind to me. "We will get you sorted," she said

I knew in my mind that I shouldn't be in this situation. Stan had a good job and he had no children with his wife. I was just his cheap bit on the side and he had dumped me at the police station!

"Where are your parents?" the officer asked.

"I don't want my mother to know," I said and started to cry again.

That night, I was transported to a huge house near the forest. It catered for the homeless and for the first time in weeks I had a good, wholesome meal. The person in charge came to talk to me and asked: "Have you been anywhere about your pregnancy, Sylvia?"

"No."

"Well, at the moment we are trying to get you a placement in a mother and baby home so we can get you sorted, but don't you worry about that. Just have a good night's sleep."

In a way, I was relieved that this police officer had taken the time and effort to help me. That night, I was given towels and night-clothes, I had a lovely bath and for the first time in months had a long, deep sleep.

When I awoke the next morning, it seemed my bulge had grown even more. I didn't feel ashamed of being pregnant but I was ashamed that I was pregnant by a married man. When I got up, I was offered a choice of breakfast. I had cereal and toast and felt that I was feeding my unborn child properly for the first time in weeks. At about 10.00am, I was informed that I would be going to a mother and baby home in Sherwood. The caring policewoman came to pick me up.

"Are you all right, Sylvia? Did you sleep okay?"

I gave her a grateful smile. "Lovely. Thanks for what you have done for me."

"Well, Sylvia, we couldn't have you walking the streets could we?"

I was very angry with Stan but on reflection I thought that maybe he had done the right thing. Mind you, he knew that he had no intention of leaving his wife, so in a way he had done this simply to save his face.

When I arrived at the mother and baby home, I was shown

around by an expectant mum and told that I was to share a bedroom with another girl named Sylvia. The woman told me there was a rota and everyone, I mean everyone, had jobs to do. At the back of the home were the owner's living quarters and the kitchen.

The lady in charge then took me to one side and we discussed my pregnancy. She told me that I had to see the doctor and she would sort my benefits out. So I did, and the doctor told me I was four and half months pregnant and that I needed a scan. I am a twin and Stan's sister had triplets, so there are multiple births on both sides. While I waited for my date to arrive, I picked up the nickname 'Twinny'.

I was soon eating as if I was having five babies and had gone from 7st to 12st. When my money got sorted out, I was able to eat properly and almost as often as I wanted. I enjoyed life a little more and as every week passed I busied myself buying for my baby [the scan had shown that I was carrying just the one].

Because I was rhesus negative, I had to be checked out and they wanted to know Stan's blood group. I had no idea and I hadn't seen him for weeks. I grew bigger and bigger and found it increasingly hard to move. Eventually, I was huge. I began to get weepy at the thought of delivering my baby alone without Stan, so I told my room-mate the situation I was in.

"He's no good to you Sylv," she said. "Dump him." Why do other people always see things so black and white? I knew it wasn't that simple.

I used to take my washing to the Bendix laundry on Haydn Road and befriended a kindly lady there who asked when my baby was due. When I told her, she said she had a pram which I could have for £5.

I was thrilled. I walked over to her home and she presented me with a pram, clothes and blanket. I thanked her and later washed them and put them away for the imminent birth.

I had been assigned a social worker who advised me to have my baby adopted.

"Look, Sylvia," she said, "adoptive parents can give the baby more."

I was heartbroken. I was determined that this baby was going to have my love and devotion. Nobody was going to take it away from me. While in the mother and baby home I had already seen a vicar's daughter have to hand her son over after loving him for six weeks. Her screams of desperation will live with me forever. Nobody was taking my babe.

Soon, there were only weeks to go before the birth and Stan had still not appeared. It had been decided that due to my blood pressure rising, the birth would be induced. Mrs Wilson, the lady taking charge of me, was my chauffeur and transported me to the City Hospital.

"Don't worry, Sylv," she said, "you will have your baby soon."

"Yes," I replied, adding quickly: "And I'm not having it adopted."

"Oh, we all know that, Sylvia. Don't you worry."

I was dropped off alone, not for the first time in my life, and was admitted to the Victoria maternity ward. Before long, the drip was fixed into my arms to start me off into labour and I knew that soon I would have my baby in my arms to love and care for.

The hours ticked by and my contractions started. The nursing auxiliary sat next to me encouraging me but I wanted Stan. I wanted the father to be near me. It should have been one of the most precious times in our lives and he wasn't there.

My contractions got worse and I was wheeled down to the labour ward. The pain was so bad that I was muttering over and over: "Never again. Never again." I had hoped that a midwife would deliver my baby and I screamed to the nurse: "I don't want a man ... I don't want a man!" but they just looked at me vacantly and before long there was a doctor present.

"It's your first child, Sylvia, you need a doctor. Don't be silly," they said when they saw how frightened I was.

Once again, I wasn't listened to but I could not stand another minute of the pain.

"Push, Sylvia, push" was soon followed by: "It's a girl!"

Suddenly, the flood gate of tears opened. My baby was handed to me and I saw that she had lovely big blue eyes and a flock of sandy coloured hair. She had a little pug nose and pink cheeks. I looked down at her perfect fingers and toes and knew that Mother Nature was wonderful.

I saw Stan in her lovely face and I wanted him so badly to see his daughter. When I was wheeled back to the ward with my babe, there was a single card from Mrs Wilson. My visitors were few and all from the mother and baby home.

AM I NOT A PERSON?

The days dragged on and eventually I left the hospital. My friend Sylvia had bought me the most gorgeous matinée coat and bonnet. I lovingly put my daughter's babygrows on with her coat and bonnet and was constantly cuddling her and stroking her lovely face. I was so happy and she was going to have my total love and devotion.

I found it very tiring being a mum, up two or three times a night feeding and changing but I loved every minute of it. It was wonderful. I hadn't decided on a name, but I had dwindled it down to two possibilities ... Carol or Lisa. The nurse had told me she was definitely not a Carol and thought Lisa would be nice. And that's the name I eventually decided on.

One day, I walked out to register her and the registrar asked me her father's name. Stan had already drilled it into my head not to have his name mentioned anywhere.

There was a silence, then "Father's name?" again.

"Oh, I don't know," was all I could say. I didn't realise that this in itself would cause me more pain and anguish.

None of my family had seen Lisa and after a few weeks I decided to pay them a visit and walked to my Aunt's in the Meadows. When I walked in, Aunty Meg picked Lisa up.

"Oh, isn't she lovely?"

I was bursting with pride. While I sat in Meg's I could smell her wonderful stew and, leaving her with Lisa, I walked into the small scullery. The smell of her carbolic soap and Lifeguard disinfectant hit my nostrils. Meg had always scrubbed her lino with carbolic. I looked in her pot sink and there were whites soaking.

"Are you staying for some stew, Sylvia?" she called through.

"Oh please!" I never needed to be asked twice about food.

"How are you, ducky?" Meg asked me. "How are you managing for money?"

Meg had always been so kind to me, giving me a shilling or two when I was desperate. As I sat eating my stew, she told me that she had informed Mum about Lisa.

"But she doesn't want to know, duck," she said. "She's disowned you."

Once again I was hurting. How on earth could Mum reject the child born to her? I knew what it was like to have a daughter and there was no way I could ever reject her.

After a while, I was to say goodbye to Meg but I knew that my visit there could prove fruitful. If Stan called, as he often did, she would be bound to tell him of my visit. I told Meg my address and 'phone number and was on my way, happy that someone did care about me and happy that I could give my babe my love and attention. So many people had suggested that I have her adopted but for once in my life I had won the argument.

I arrived back at the mother and baby home and carried out my jobs according to the rota. It was my turn for the potato peeling. I was feeding Lisa when the 'phone rang.

"Sylvia Charles, it's for you."

I ran to the 'phone and yes, sure enough, it was Stan. My little plan had worked.

"Hello, duck. Where have you been?"

I yelled at him: "When I was in labour I needed you so much to hold my hand."

"But you know I don't like hospitals, Sylvia."

"Some excuse," I muttered. "But I tell you what, Stan, I have never ever been so happy. Thanks for giving me the most precious thing in my life, my daughter. Are you coming over?"

"When?"

"Now!"

I wanted so much for him to see his first child and he told me he would be in Sherwood in one hour. I was thrilled! I asked my friend to baby-sit while I got ready and went to meet him.

I put my coat on excitedly, cramming a bag of crisps into my mouth at the same time. I eat when I'm happy and I eat when I'm sad. I came out and looked down the fog-bound street, happy to see Stan waiting there. I got into his car and he gave me a cuddle.

"You look well, ducky. I have missed you."

"I'm tired," I said, trying to make him feel guilty over not playing the father role. Then I added: "I'm going to fetch Lisa."

"No, no, Sylv, don't," he said. "It's too cold."

But before he could say anything else, I was gone. I wrapped Lisa up in a warm shawl, held her close to my body and walked back to Stan. He opened the door and when I sat down we made eye-to-eye contact.

Then he looked down and I handed him this little miracle of nature with her pug nose peeping through the shawl. Stan took hold of her hand and for the first time I saw him cry.

AM I NOT A PERSON?

"Oh Sylv, Sylv, I'm choked. You have given me something I have always wanted."

I knew Stan was probably in his forties and had seen a lot more of the world than I had, but I knew he felt humbled at this moment. As he cradled Lisa, he reached over to kiss me but I froze. I wanted to be one happy family, not Stan's sex toy. I was only with him a few minutes because my babe was getting cold.

After we said our goodbyes, I walked back, glancing around to wave to Stan as he disappeared into the foggy distance. That night, when I went to bed, I asked myself over and over how Mum could have neglected me. Why didn't she love me like I loved Lisa? I settled Lisa down and started to sob.

Once again, I was in the dark and the shadows of the night brought fear back into my life … the haunting eyes of the past. While I lay there crying, my friend came into my room.

"What's upset you, Sylv?"

"Nothing," I lied. "I just feel a little weepy, that's all."

I was hurting so badly inside but my torture was in silence. Nobody knew of my past.

Even though I was happy with Lisa, the flashbacks continued to haunt me and I found the pain almost too much to bear. My eating was now way out of control. Every waking hour I was thinking about food.

Chapter 10

Married to the wrong man

The pain, the rejection, was there for me,
What I had done wrong is a mystery.

The weeks went on and I found Mum's rejection of Lisa and me more and more difficult to comprehend. I wanted Mummy to want me and there was a hole inside that I just couldn't fill, no matter how much I ate.

When Lisa was five months old, I decided to walk to the Elbow Café on Mansfield Road which used to cater for the 'ordinary' people of Nottingham. I knew Mum would be there. I lovingly dressed Lisa in her white brushed nylon dress that I had bought for under £1 and put her best frilly pillowcase in the pram. I arrived at the café not knowing what reaction I would face.

"Oh hello, Sylvia," said Mum's friend who came across to me. Then she saw Lisa. "Isn't she gorgeous?"

She picked Lisa up and cuddled her. My babe was all smiles.

"Mary, come over and see Lisa," Mum's friend said, but Mum didn't even acknowledge us.

Mum's friend pushed half a crown into Lisa's hand, gave me a sympathetic smile, and I was on my way.

As I pushed the pram up Mansfield Road, my hurt turned into rage. Mum had rejected my child as well as me. I started to shout: "I hate you, I hate you!" not caring who would hear me.

When I arrived back at the mother and baby home, there was a message. Stan had rung. I supposed that he wanted my body again and, sure enough, he said he had decided he wasn't seeing enough of me.

"Why don't you get a flat, Sylv?"

"Why Stan? I'm happy here."

But I knew I couldn't stay at the mother and baby home forever, so I would have to make a move soon. Within a matter of days, Stan had found me a one-bedroomed place which was very basic - bed, lino and curtains - and very, very lonely.

AM I NOT A PERSON?

I just couldn't handle the loneliness and every time Stan came to see me, I started to cry: "I need you, Stan."

The fear of the past was ever present. The room reminded me so much of where I was raped and I was really scared. I just didn't feel safe in this flat. Yes, I had my darling Lisa but I found the loneliness too much to handle.

A few weeks on and Stan found me another flat, this time in a huge bay-fronted house with its own kitchen. The family downstairs were extremely poor but very friendly. We would share our neck of lamb stew and roast breast of lamb.

I had no furniture or anything of my own, so Stan brought an old army coat round one day to protect my body from the cold at night. Many times, I would just lay on the bed looking at my precious little girl. Even though I'd had a tortuous childhood, I was grateful that God had blessed me with my perfect babe.

At times, though, I felt so alone and Stan would just keep turning up for brief spells, having sex with me then going back to his wife. I wanted so desperately to play happy families. He said he called round at every opportunity but I started to feel more and more like a prostitute.

I hated myself for my inability to stop this form of abuse by Stan and I hated what was causing it ... my body. So I began to mutilate myself under my bed covers, scratching my private parts constantly until they bled. I also started hacking at my wrists, the blood flowing out a way of cleansing myself from the poisons in my body. My babe was the only thing that kept me going through all my inner torment.

Some Caribbean people had moved next door and their eyes haunted me whenever I saw them. It seemed like they were looking at me every time that I stepped out.

By the October of 1967 I was moving on, where I didn't know, I just had to get out. I packed my few belongings and once again made my way to my Aunt's in the Meadows. Meg loved Lisa and would spoil her. By now, Lisa was beginning to take notice of people and her vivid blue eyes and smile would melt anyone's heart.

I found out that Mum had moved into the Meadows, about 10 minutes walk away, just off Meadow Lane. I was desperate for us to be a family, for Mum to want us and to feel safe. After all, Lisa was Mum's grandchild. I knew I would possibly be hurt by taking Lisa to see Mum, but I was willing to take that chance.

AM I NOT A PERSON?

I passed by the Notts County football ground and walked up to Mum's house, a back-to-back terrace. Then I started to feel a little frightened of the reaction I would get. I still had no idea why Mum had neglected me and I dreamed of the day she and I could be close. Just for her to give me a kiss and say "Sorry" would have healed some of my pain.

When I knocked on the door, I felt a sense of panic. What if she told me to go? I don't think I could have handled it. I waited but there no answer. I gave up and decided to visit a friend who lived nearby.

Her home was very cosy and when I explained that I was homeless she kindly invited me to stay. I paid my way and, while I was grateful for her offering me digs which helped me out for a while, I knew I couldn't live there forever.

One day, after going to Mum's and finding her out for the umpteenth time, I walked to the shop and bought a pack of Jammy Doughnuts. I crammed them into my mouth as if it was a race against time but it didn't take away the pain. I decided there and then that I would hatch a plan to try to get Mum to want me.

I walked to the Trent embankment and spread Lisa's blanket on the step. I held her on my knee and threw little pebbles into the river. When they hit the water, the ripples got bigger and bigger just as my plan began to take shape. I knew Mum's favourite flowers were tulips and, although my money situation was not fantastic, I managed to buy some bunches. I put them together and tied a big red bow around them. Then I attached a card that read: "To Mum, love Sylvia and Lisa" and left them on her doorstep. But I still heard nothing. My plan had failed.

Soon, Lisa had grown into an 11 month toddler. She was no longer just a babe, she was becoming a person. The urge to see Mum was with me every day. I wanted her to accept Lisa even if she couldn't accept me. I decided one more time to walk to Mum's and on the way ate several Mars bars and a few cheese biscuits to make myself feel better. I got to her door, knocked on it and it suddenly opened. Standing there was Mum!

"Look who I've brought to see you," I said.

She stared at me and that familiar coldness scared me for a moment. Then she looked down at Lisa, with her blue eyes and grin showing her front teeth off. I watched Mum stoop to pick Lisa up and saw her heart melt. She cuddled her then asked us

AM I NOT A PERSON?

in. The house was very unkempt and pets were everywhere ... cats, hamsters, gerbils ... plus a mountain of ash in the hearth, but it was home.

"How are you, Diana?" she asked, not looking me in the face.

But I was pleased to be sitting in Mum's home. I had been banished from her life for so long.

"I'm looking for a flat, Mum."

She didn't answer me and just fussed Lisa. She even took her trinket box out for her to play with. Lisa had her white socks on and before long they were grubby but that didn't matter to me. I was where I belonged, home with Mum, and for a while I was happy, happy that Lisa was going to grow up to know her Nan.

After about an hour or so, I heard somebody coming downstairs. I looked around and there, standing at the back of me, was my sister. She was nine years younger than me and I really didn't know her. But what I did know was that she had been spoiled rotten by Mum. She seemed jealous of Lisa and I felt uneasy.

I was about to leave when Stan knocked on Mum's door. His magical antennae had managed to find me again. His face lit up when he saw Lisa and me.

"There's a terraced house going, Sylv."

"Where, where?" I asked.

"Kinglake Place, off Wilford Road. You know where Alice lives don't you? Would you like it?"

"Can you pull some strings?"

"We will have to see Sylv," Stan said, then added: "I've got the name of the estate agents. Come on, let's get the keys."

I picked Lisa up, put her dummy in, said goodbye to Mum, put Lisa in the back of Stan's Morris 1000 and got into the front.

"Do you want me to stop at the chippy, duck?" Stan enquired.

He knew what the answer would be.

"Fish, chips and peas, please!"

I was so happy, happy that my Mum had given Lisa a love. So, I ate while Lisa slept. I sat stuffing my face while Stan went to the estate agents for the keys. Then, suddenly, he was in front of the car, jiggling the keys with a grin on his face.

My heart was skipping a beat at the thought of my own home. Not only that, but in the same row as my best mate, Connie. By the time we arrived, Lisa had woken up but she didn't cry. Maybe she was as eager to see inside the house as I was!

We went in and there was an echo because there were no furnishings in the house, just the basics. It was a two-bedroomed house with an outside loo and a coalhouse. But I didn't really care what it looked like. It would be my first real home.

"Well duck, do you want it?"

"Yes, Stan, Yes. When can I move in?"

"Give me a few days. I'm sure I will get it."

When I was sitting in Aunty Meg's a couple of days later, Stan arrived.

"Here you are, duck," he said and gave me the keys. The house was in his name and he paid the fortnightly rent of £150. Stan was a welder and earned a fantastic wage working on big power stations. He was also on danger money.

Around this time, on one of my visits to Meg's, Stan introduced me to Bill, a bit of a loner who seemed to want to confide in me about his past. He seemed harmless enough. For some reason, Stan encouraged me to see him and persuaded me to let him help with the move into Kinglake Place.

The day arrived when I was to move in. All I had was my suitcase and Lisa's crib that I'd decorated myself with lead-free paint and stickers. But it was my home. I raised enough money for a bag of pre-pack coal and I lit the fire and sat on my suitcase. My home. I was thrilled. Stan had heard about somebody doing a moonlight flit across the road, leaving behind an old spring bed and a very old cooker. He fetched them for me and Bill, Connie and myself busied ourselves cleaning the grime off. It was an old mottled green cooker and it had layers of grease on it.

I so desperately wanted him to move in so that we could be one happy family, but he wouldn't.

"Build a relationship with Bill," Stan kept saying to me, but I was angry inside. The man I loved was not moving in with me and I was being made to mix with someone I didn't care for.

Why did Stan want this relationship? Basically, because he had his home comforts and a marriage and didn't want to face up to fatherhood.

He also believed that it would be easy to get Bill out of the way whenever Stan wanted his sexual thrills.

AM I NOT A PERSON?

I realised right from the start that I simply couldn't build a relationship with Bill but Stan kept saying: "Sylv, he's all right, he's not violent."

He also threatened me with Aston Hall if I didn't go along with what he said. He knew that my label was following me and just one word from him could see me back within those oppressive walls. I was being manipulated and brainwashed all the time by Stan but nobody else knew anything about it.

When Lisa was two, I found myself pregnant once again. Stan was worried. He wanted to have sex and he wanted babies but as for being a full-time dad, that was a totally different story. So, this man, who I loved dearly, decided to arrange that I marry Bill. I was heartbroken and confused but knew in my heart even then that Stan would not desert me. The wedding was arranged for the summer of 1969, by which time I was five months pregnant. I borrowed a white wedding dress from Connie.

I had managed to furnish my house and even though a lot of the furniture had come from the Family First trust, it was quite comfortable. But I began to feel like a slave. Despite the fact that I was to be married in a week's time and I was heavily pregnant, Stan called for his usual bout of sex. But instead of giving in and letting him have his way, I turned on him.

"No Stan," I said, "you're not using me anymore."

He looked at me with amazement.

"Why don't you tell me, Sylv? You're having it with Bill."

"Don't be ridiculous!" I spluttered. "I don't love him, Stan, I love you!"

There was a silence. Then I walked into the kitchen and broke down. Why was I in this position? I classed myself as an intelligent human being and here I was being used.

Three days before the wedding, Connie and I went shopping but I was a total wreck. I kept breaking down. Connie thought it was pre-wedding nerves but in reality I didn't want to marry Bill. That same day, Stan called. He said he loved me and that the wedding would only be for a short while, then we would be together. I believed him.

The day arrived. Connie had dressed Lisa up and I had put my wedding dress on. Stan arrived in his car with ribbons on the bonnet. He had his grey suit on and it showed off his blue eyes.

73

AM I NOT A PERSON?

When he came to the door, I sobbed: "I'm not going through with it. You can't force me."

"Come on, duck, it won't be for long."

He drove me to Shakespeare Street where there were more of Stan's relatives than mine waiting outside. The wedding was over quickly and we all went home.

I knew my life was being ruined again, this time by a different kind of abuse. After a few weeks, I found I was unable to relate at all to Bill and I was constantly on at Stan until one day I just snapped. I felt like I couldn't take any more.

"You should make a commitment to me and your daughter," I yelled at Stan, "and the child I am carrying!"

I dug my marriage certificate out of my handbag and threw it on to the fire. Stan just sat there and didn't utter a word.

I was distraught but I lived in hope that one day, just one day soon, I would have Stan in my life for good.

Chapter 11

The birth and death of a child

You were dancing as you disappeared from view,
I looked down at the grass and saw the dew
Shining and glistening like a jewel.
As I looked closer for you I knew
That your spirit was shining through.
The emptiness, the despair I feel
Will take forever to heal.

A few months later, I decided to decorate my house. I was proud my daughter and I had our home, even though it was small and the loo was outside. I was so proud that I even decorated that and put a carpet in it.

Lisa was a good child and she had my undivided love. I also got help from Connie who on many occasions would give Lisa dinners because she knew my finances were not very good.

A major problem I had at this time was having to explain to Bill that I was pregnant. After all, we had never had a sexual relationship. What if he threw me out when I told him? Yet again, I felt threatened and vulnerable.

One day, I was busying myself, stripping the walls of the living room - it was only 10' by 10' so it didn't take long - while the aroma of corned beef stew on my antique cooker filtered in from the kitchen.

Bill had had his skin full of beer at the local pub and when he arrived home he was full of himself.

"'ello, Sylv, duck, what's for dinner?"

"Can't you smell it?" I replied. "Corned beef stew."

I *had* to tell him.

"Bill," I began, "before you have your dinner I've got something to tell you." As quick as a flash I added: "I'm pregnant," and waited for his reaction.

I didn't have to wait long. Bill immediately jumped up in the air as if something had bitten him and then just as quickly sat down on my old, dilapidated cottage suite.

"Sylv, you're pregnant! Well done gel," he said.

AM I NOT A PERSON?

I was confused. How could he be overjoyed that I was going to have a baby when we had had no sexual contact? But that was Bill's only reaction. Minutes later, he was sitting down to a dish of piping hot corned beef stew and loving every mouthful.

As the weeks and months went by, my attention for Lisa was paramount. I was determined that she should never feel neglected or live in a dirty home.

So I carried on decorating the walls of my house using cheap wallpaper from the shop at the end of Kinglake Place. I would also scrub my tatty old lino with Fairy soap and Dettol.

I often felt quite ill over the second pregnancy and I knew something was not right. On my first trip to the hospital, my assumptions proved to be spot on.

I was told that I would have to be kept in during the weeks leading up to the birth and that the baby's life could be at risk. I immediately burst out crying, not for me but for my daughter.

"What about Lisa?!" I sobbed. I couldn't bear to be parted from her. My darling Lisa had had my love and devotion all these months.

My friend offered to look after Lisa while I was away but it wouldn't be the same. No disrespect to Connie, but she wasn't me. Although she said: "She'll be all right, Sylv", I knew that Connie had no children of her own. I dropped Lisa off at Connie's before I was admitted and it pulled at my heartstrings. She was my life.

In hospital, I was so ill that I was assigned a side room and given drugs to reduce my blood pressure. I knew that my precious baby's life was in danger. I knew that I was in danger of dying as well.

On Christmas Eve, I was moved to the maternity ward. While drifting in and out of my drug induced sleep, I heard the angelic voices of the nurses singing on the ward. For a few moments I really did think I was in heaven … until I ran my hand over my stomach and felt an enormous bulge.

Even at this stage, I wished in my heart that I could be with my darling Lisa. After all, Santa should be coming to her that night and I was stuck in this hospital.

As I lay there, the nursing staff came to check my blood pressure again. There was great concern at what they saw and I was sedated one more time to try to save my unborn child.

On 27 December, it was decided that my baby's birth should

be brought forward. As I lay under the starched white sheets, I sensed an urgency around me. The staff came to check my name tag, then they started to push my bed. Again, I had the overpowering feeling that something was wrong.

"What's the matter, nurse?"

"Nothing, Sylvia. Nothing to worry about," she replied. "We're just going to break your membranes to start you off in labour. Your consultant thinks it's best for you and the baby."

In a way, I was relieved that it was about to happen. Relieved that the lump on my stomach would soon be gone, relieved that I could see an end to my stay in hospital ... but especially relieved that I would soon be with my darling Lisa once more.

As I entered the labour ward, I began to tremble through past experience and I hoped a midwife would break my water. I was wheeled into a room which was full of equipment. My bed was put alongside another one so that I could shuffle my body on to it and I lay there for what seemed like a very long time.

I looked up to see a contraption that resembled stirrups and then a male doctor arrived. I was screaming inside, shouting in my mind: "Go away! I need a midwife!" But I remained silent. The fear had paralysed my vocal chords.

Breaking the membrane must have only taken a few seconds but it seemed much longer. Afterwards, I was taken to a dark room and fitted with a drip. Then, when my labour had progressed, I was wheeled back into the delivery room.

"Sylvia," I heard a voice say, "your baby's a brow presentation." Then I heard the doctor describe to his staff that a birth like this is one in a million.

As my pains became more and more intense, I desperately wanted Stan by my side to hold my hand. I was screaming so loud: "The pain, the pain!" I was encouraged to push and I really thought my blood vessels were going to burst.

"Sylvia, one big push."

Then I felt my baby come out.

"It's a boy, Sylvia. It's a boy!"

I burst out crying. I wanted Stan. I needed him now more than ever to see his son.

It seemed an age before I was handed my son and when I looked at him I saw Mother Nature's miracle. But almost instantly, I began to realise that things weren't right.

"Nurse, what's wrong with his head?"

AM I NOT A PERSON?

"It's your delivery, love, you had a very difficult birth."

As I cradled him, his hands seemed to tremble. Was it withdrawal symptoms from the drugs he had absorbed while he was inside me? The doctor came over and told me my baby had to go into the Special Care Baby Unit. I started to cry and the nurse put her arm around me.

"Look, love, he will only be there for a while. You can visit him as soon as we have washed you down."

Within minutes, the nurse brought me a bowl and I used my flannel. I felt absolutely exhausted. The long birth had taken its toll on me. But tired as I was, I began to throw a tantrum.

"I want to see him!"

"Wait until we get some more staff on." The Special Care Baby Unit was the place he should be, I was assured of that.

Shortly, I was wheeled to visit him and saw his rosy cheeks peeping out over his blanket. His little head looked so odd to me but my main concern when I went back to my ward and bed was how Lisa would accept her new brother. He was so much like Stan.

I didn't want Bill to visit, I wanted his dad to see him. I was so proud and excited that I now had a boy and a lovely girl to give my love to. All I wanted was for Stan to be with us.

After a day or two, my son was back at my bedside and Connie had brought Lisa to see her new brother. She accepted him straight away. Connie had put a big ribbon in Lisa's beautiful blonde hair and she had her lovely new shoes on. I was so happy. For the first time in my life, I was actually content. To be truthful, I felt quite giddy. I had given birth to two beautiful children.

But my happiness was not to last because on the day I was released from hospital, Bill came to pick me up. I wanted Stan so desperately to show me how happy he was at the fact that he had a son.

As I dressed my son to come home, I lovingly tickled his chin and he gave me a smile. The white maternity coat I put on him was Lisa's. "It's nice to share," I said to Lisa, who was now two years old.

When I arrived home with my new baby, Bill kept fussing around. John, who was living with us for a short while, said with a grin: "You're made now, Sylv. One of each. Can't be bad, can it?"

AM I NOT A PERSON?

Bill was going to work thrilled about me having a boy. But surely he must have known the child wasn't his!?

Lisa and Connie had made up my blue coach-built pram with pale blue sheets and blankets, especially for my new boy. Our house was very damp so I also kept the coal fire on 24 hours a day. Even though this was eating into my resources, it was worth it to keep everybody warm.

I decided we would have a vote on my son's name but before I knew it my twin said "Robert" and it seemed just perfect.

I wanted to show my son off to the world and Lisa helped me to put a seat on the pram. When we walked to the shops, I would ask her: "Is Robert asleep?"

"Mum, asleep," she'd say and point to Robert.

She never got jealous, but then she had no reason to. I loved her as much as Robert and made her feel just as important. She even helped me to change his nappies.

At the age of six weeks, Robert had to go to the hospital, again to the Special Care Baby Unit. Lisa came with me and we were called into a cubicle.

"Undress Robert," I was told, which wasn't easy because he was a lively lad.

As I did so, the nurse was busy measuring his head.

"Why are you doing that?" I had a gut feeling they were hiding something from me.

"How has Robert been, love?"

"Oh, he's been well but he has had a cold for weeks."

"Well, we will take a swab."

"What's wrong with his head?" I asked bluntly.

"Nothing, love, he had a difficult birth."

I was assured everything was fine but mother's instinct or something told me something was definitely wrong. When I got on the bus home, I showed him off but people looked at him as though he was deformed. But he was my baby and I loved him no matter what his head was like.

I wanted Mum to see him and, as if by some fluke, she arrived at my house not long after I had come back from the hospital. Stan had turned up as well.

"Here you are Mum, your grandson."

When she held him, she said: "He's just like a little old man."

I was hurt. "It's my baby you're talking about," I said. Then there was a deathly silence.

79

AM I NOT A PERSON?

Even though I always kept Robert in the warmth, something told me he was not well. His nose was running and his bottles were not getting drunk. I decided to call the doctor out.

"What's wrong Mrs ------?" he asked me.

"Well, as you can see his nose is running."

"You're whittling too much over this child," he said. "There's nothing wrong with him."

But a mother's instinct is so powerful, I knew things weren't right. A few days later, I noticed when I changed his bottom before settling him down that he seemed listless. I stoked the fire and put him into his pram. I didn't dare take him upstairs because it was too damp. In fact, the wallpaper hung from the walls, even though I had recently decorated my room.

I pulled the hood up on the pram and winded Robert, then I gave him a goodnight kiss as I did with Lisa. I went to bed knowing Robert was warm and I always left the stair door and bedroom door open so I could listen out for him. Robert was going between three and four hours between his feeds and I went to bed feeling happy, happy that I had my little house and my two children. I eventually fell into a kind of cat nap.

Robert had a strong pair of lungs and would cry so loud my neighbours could hear him. But as I rolled over in my bed that night, I realised there hadn't been a sound from him for some time. How long had I been asleep? I instantly leapt out of bed and ran down the narrow staircase. I fell down the last three and landed on the floor.

"What are you doing, Sylv?" asked John, who had been roused by the noise I had made.

He helped me up and as I approached Robert's pram, I seemed to know something was wrong. I pulled the blankets back and leaned over to pick Robert up. When I touched him I literally jumped back.

"No, no, he can't be!" I screamed. "John, John, he's dead. He's dead!"

Robert was limp and cold and all I was do in blind panic was keep on screaming: "He's dead! He's dead!"

John ran down to get Connie who came rushing in.

"Connie, Connie, he's dead," I said, stamping my feet. "Help me, please help me."

Connie took Lisa to her house and I screamed at my twin: "John, fetch Stan!"

AM I NOT A PERSON?

Before I realised what was happening, an ambulance had arrived. "Where is he love?"

"He's there," I said, pointing to the pram. I had started to shake from head to foot. Was this real? Or was I still cat napping and having a terrible dream?

"It can't be," I kept repeating while the ambulance men looked at Robert. "It can't be."

"Calm down Mrs ------, we need to talk to you," the ambulance man said, but I could only scream: "He's mine, he's mine!"

"Mrs ------, your son is dead."

"No, no, he's not," I yelled. I was shaking my head. "He's not!"

"I'm sorry, but there's nothing more we can do for him."

The ambulance man left me and walked back towards the pram while his mate spread a blanket on the settee which I knew was hard and stenched a little. The ambulance man went to pick Robert out of the pram and I jumped up.

"You're not taking him!" I said but he bypassed me and all I could see was my baby, my baby held up to lay on the blanket. He put him on the settee and I realised he was going to take him away.

"You can't take him. He's mine!" I said. "No, you're not taking him!" I yelled and yelled but to no avail. I followed the men outside to the ambulance, all the while screaming: "Please, please, don't take him!"

John came over to me. "Come on, Sylv."

When the ambulance started to pull away I hung on to the doors, screaming: "No! No!" The ambulance stopped and I opened the door.

I tried to snatch Robert back. "He's mine. Don't you realise? He's my baby."

There was silence from everyone. They didn't know what to do and the air was filled with my screams and sobs.

"Come on, Sylvia," said John. "Stan's here." I sobbed and sobbed as John took me into the house where Stan was sitting on the settee looking solemn.

"Where were you!?" I screamed at him. "My baby's dead!"

"It was meant to be, Sylv," was all he said.

I took the wedding picture of me and Bill off the wall and smashed it on Stan's head.

AM I NOT A PERSON?

"I need you!" I screamed. "I need you!"

No amount of Stan's voice saying it was meant to be could take away my grief, my anger and a feeling of desperation. Everything had happened in minutes and before long I was being questioned by police in my own home on the circumstances leading up to Robert's death. John made me a coffee and Stan tried to console me. When the officer wanted to take statements asking how Robert was found, I was of no use.

"How can I remember?" I screamed. "I love him, I want him."

"Now Mrs ------," the officer persevered, "Robert is dead. How did you find him?"

I couldn't remember what position I found him in. All I knew was that I got up to check on him and he was cold.

A statement was taken from John and within minutes the police left. As I sat there crying, I looked up. "Robert's there, look," I said. I swore I saw him move in the pram. I got up and just sat there holding his lovely soft blue blanket. Everybody thought I was mad. I went to bed and took his blanket with me.

"Sylv, don't be stupid," Bill told me as I sat there, day in, day out, holding the blanket close to me. "Let's get rid of the pram. It reminds you too much."

"Why shouldn't I be reminded of him? He's my son!"

"I know Sylv, but it makes you cry too much," Bill said in a caring sort of way, but I wasn't interested and I told him to shut up. He had no understanding that I needed Robert's things around me so that I could feel close. I would regularly walk around with a piece of Robert's blanket stuffed inside my bra.

Connie told me to go down to her place if I ever felt bad. She was minding Lisa who was being so good for her. Connie understood how shocked I was. Nothing was too much for her and she offered to have Lisa until after Robert's funeral.

Bill seemed to look worried when I got back home. Stan had turned up and they had clearly both been up to something. When I walked into the lounge I glanced into the corner and saw that Robert's pram had gone. I let out an almighty scream.

"What's wrong, Sylv?" asked Bill.

"It's gone, it's gone. My baby's pram's gone."

"Stan took everything away to stop you thinking about Robert," he said.

"You bastard, you bastard!" I screamed at Stan. As I cried, he told me that I really should go to visit Robert in hospital, where he was until an inquest was carried out.

But my mind was telling me he was still alive. Everything around me was a fog. I couldn't register on any task. One day, when Connie was sitting with me, I said:

"Are you coming with me, Connie?"

She looked me up and down. "Where to Sylv?"

"To see Robert." My eyes filled with tears.

"Sylv, he's not with us any more."

"I know Connie, but I'm going to visit him at Lymms."

I had decided to wear black clothes to respect my son. I wanted everyone to know that I was in mourning. I wanted them to know the pain that I was experiencing.

"I don't really want to go," Connie said, "but I will, Sylv, to support you."

On the day I was to visit, we all got ready in total silence, then walked down the road to catch the bus. One of my neighbours came out as we passed.

"Sorry, love, to hear about your baby," she said and I burst out crying. Between the sobs, I blurted out that I was going to visit him and she walked away, shaking her head as if I was mad. Many of the other neighbours would just cross the road whenever they saw me. It was as if I had some kind of plague.

Mum had called to see me that morning but there was no sympathy, just harsh words to tell me she was also going to see Robert. I told her I was taking a bunch of forget-me-nots to place on Robert which I had dressed with a beautiful white bow, but I was not prepared for what confronted me when I saw Robert.

When we got to Lymms on Bath Street in Sneinton, Nottingham, Connie said she would wait in the Chapel of Rest while I visited Robert. "I'm not going to see him, Sylv."

"Oh Connie, don't be like that, please. Please."

But she stayed in the waiting room with Lisa. I opened the door of the Chapel of Rest with the flowers in my hand and froze. Was this reality or a nightmare? Robert's coffin was lined with white silk and there, there lying lifeless was my baby, with a bunch of forget-me-nots already on him. I couldn't believe it. I walked to the coffin, stood over Robert and ran my hands on his satin gown which soon became wet from my tears.

"Oh, Mum, why have you done this to me? Why?" She had

been to see Robert before me, knowing that I was taking forget-me-nots, and had placed a bunch of the very same flowers on him. I know Mum had not been a tower of strength to me over the soul destroying years, but now she was hurting me beyond belief. And at a time in my life when I needed her more than ever.

I stood there for what seemed an age just stroking Robert's face. Then I knelt down to say a silent prayer when a so-called friend arrived. I had not seen her for years but the news about Robert had obviously travelled. Suddenly, she started to pull Robert's gown away to look at his feet.

"What are you doing?"

"I'm trying to look at his feet. Do you know, Sylv, they don't care how they stitch them up."

I felt dizzy and the next thing I remember I was sitting down in the corridor. This was turning into a complete nightmare and the world seemed to have gone totally insane.

I needed to see Robert every day before the funeral ... before he left me for good ... and the next time I went I took my camera. I realised I didn't have one photo of my baby and I took several because I needed something to treasure. But none of them came out. They say God works in mysterious ways.

The thought of not being able to see Robert any more was tearing me apart. As every day passed, I knew that the final goodbye was getting closer. At this time, I had developed a rash all over my body that looked as if I had measles. It must have been a nervous reaction or something.

My mind and body were being destroyed by the whole situation ... not only what I had been through over the years and what was happening with Stan and Bill, but the unbeliev-able pain of losing Robert and now having to make the funeral arrangements. I felt so alone. Oh Mum, why weren't you there when I needed you?

I wanted to do the very best for Robert but we were on the poverty line and I didn't have an insurance policy for him. How on earth was I going to bury him?

I had discussed it with Stan and he was at a loss what to do, so I decided to go to Citizen's Advice to ask for their help. Connie went with me to the plush offices on Shakespeare Street. The man in the thick, dark rimmed glasses told me that I could claim for the funeral off Bill's insurance but I was very angry at the thought of having to do this. The father of Robert should have paid but he didn't seem to be interested, even though he certainly had the money.

Then the man asked: "Would you like your son buried or cremated, Mrs ------?"

"No," I sobbed. "I don't want him burned. I want him buried."

"I'm sorry, but you can't have him buried."

I looked at him confused. Why had he asked me if I had no choice?

"Burial is too expensive," he explained, as if in response to my facial expression.

How I wished I had the money but there was no chance. I was so heartbroken and I didn't stop crying for days at the thought of my son being burned. How could they do this to him?

The night before the funeral, I made a plan. I decided I would take Robert from Lymms to my house and keep him forever in my bedroom. I wandered up to Lymms, constantly asking why babies have to die. I got there at about 2.00am and sat on Bath Street Park wall, looking into the window. I walked over to the doors but I knew they would be locked. I knew they would stop me seeing my child. So I wandered back home and cried and cried. I knew that tomorrow would be the last time I would ever see him.

Connie had Lisa the following day because she found it too distressing to go to funerals, let alone one for a nine-week-old baby. Bill was rushing around like a headless chicken and I was hardly in a state of composure. He saw me tuck part of Robert's blanket down my bra and snatched it off me. I was hysterical. The only bit of Robert I had!

He walked off down the road with it and I ran after him screaming: "Bring it back!" but I never saw it again. Ten minutes before the hearse arrived and I was in a right state. How could he do this to me?

I desperately wanted the father of my baby with me but he followed behind in his car. To his credit, Bill tried to console me when I was placed in the car that would follow Robert but I felt numb and hurt. Once again, my heart was breaking. This time I had been pushed to the limit.

When we arrived at the Chapel in Wilford, Mum was already

there. No arm reaching out to me, just a coldness. The funeral service is a haze in my memory. All I could see was my baby placed at the front of the Chapel. I whispered to whoever was near me: "The lid's on - he won't be able to breathe."

"He's dead, love," they said. "He's gone to a better place."

I couldn't even have a special casket. Finances would not permit.

As we sang our hymns, I noticed the golden gates closing and whispered: "Suffer little children to come unto me". My eyes were overflowing with tears and when I knelt down to pray I swear I heard the coffin drop. I stood up and let out an almighty scream. It was so final. I would never see him again.

Robert's ashes were sprinkled over the garden of rest and I went home. I needed Mum so much but she had gone back to her own house without saying a word. I didn't even have Robert's square of blanket to hold close to me - that had gone as well.

While I stood there in a daze, Connie said something to me that cut even deeper.

"Sylv, malicious gossip has started."

"What do you mean?"

"Well, one of the neighbours is saying that you suffocated Robert."

I started to sob hysterically. This was the final straw. Why were they doing this to me? I ran upstairs to get the death certificate and some Sellotape.

When I came back down, Connie asked: "What are you doing?"

"I'm sticking this death certificate in the window," I said, "and for every face that comes to look at it I will be staring right back at them."

[Editor's note: the death certificate states that Robert died of bronchial pneumonia and congestion of the lungs]

Chapter 12

Bingeing in Bestwood

Food controls my life.
"Don't eat like that," Stan yells.
"What is it to do with you?" I yell back
Shovelling the food in at a rapid pace
As if I'm in some sort of race.

After Robert's death, I lost control. I started bingeing constantly to the point of eating frozen food straight out of the freezer.

Connie was having Lisa for me more and more. She even took her away for weekends. But she shocked me when she said that she was moving away from the district, out to Forest Fields. I was upset but at the end of the day, Connie had her own life to lead and she had given me so much help over the years.

She told me to visit her anytime but I knew that this would not be possible because I was conscious of my increasing size. I was ever more wary of opening the door to people and even when Stan called he started to shout at me. My weight had gone up to 18st. One good thing, I thought, maybe now no man will want to look at me.

Shortly after Connie's move, we were informed that our houses were to be demolished and we would be allocated council accommodation. Many houses where we lived were already boarded up.

We received our letter from the Nottingham City Council and Stan and Bill took Lisa to look at the new house. I was becoming such a recluse and I found it impossible to get a bus, so I didn't go with them. When they came back, Bill said: "It's lovely, Sylv. Massive gardens."

"I will see it when we move," I said, and before long I was busy packing. I had happy and sad memories in my little house and the day we moved I glanced back at it with a tear in my eye. It was the ending of another chapter in my life.

We moved on to a huge council estate called the Bestwood

AM I NOT A PERSON?

Estate and it wasn't long before I was pregnant by Stan for the third time. Once again, I was very ill and had to be hospitalised for weeks. Despite the distance, Connie proved what a good friend she was and took care of Lisa.

I had another son by Caesarean section and named him Mark. Bill had to look after me when I came home but I really hated my life; it was a complete sham. I was living in my silent world of pain ... pain of the past and the pain of being used as a sex object by Stan. There was never any concern for what I wanted or how I felt. My life had become hell.

Stan would call on me every lunchtime to get his sexual kicks. He had just 30 minutes to get to my house, have sex with me, then run back to work. Why was I letting this happen?

Sometimes, Connie would call unexpectedly and I would have to open the door to let her in while Stan slipped out of another. I was racked with guilt about my situation because Connie didn't know that Stan was the father of my children. What would she think of me going with a man 30 years my senior?

When Mark was five months old, I found myself expecting Stan's fourth child.

"I don't want another baby, Stan," I sobbed. "I can't cope with another."

When the health visitor called to see Lisa, Mark and me, Lisa was playing happily in her toy room which I had decorated for her with great love and care with Postman Pat paper. It used to be a coalhouse and I had turned it into her toy room with a big window in it. It wasn't long before I was given a doctor's appointment and by the time I arrived I was a complete wreck. I was in such a state. My name was called but I just sat in the doctor's surgery and started to cry.

When I eventually went in to see the doctor, I said: "I don't want another baby."

"Well, Mrs ------, I'm afraid you cannot have an abortion. But we will give you all the help you need with this baby."

I kept my first ante-natal appointment but I didn't feel I could cope with spending another long period in hospital. I would have to leave my adorable children, with Bill doing the shopping and taking the kids to school. To the outside world, we must have seemed a normal, happy family but inside the four walls of our house it was absolute torture.

AM I NOT A PERSON?

Stan had so much to answer for and he still would not make a commitment as a father. I felt it was his duty to come to me now at this time, especially when my worst fears became reality. It was decided that I needed to be hospitalised because the placenta was before the baby. I was assigned a social worker from the City Hospital who asked me what my family situation was like.

"I have no-one," I said. "They are all in Australia."

I didn't want Bill to look after my children and the only relative I had locally was John, who at this time lived in a multi-storey flat in Basford. He had offered to have Mark and my friend would have Lisa.

The social worker told me that if these arrangements failed, she would be able to arrange foster care for my children. I was reassured by this but at the same time I was hurt, hurt that Stan had allowed this situation to carry on. Didn't he have any feelings for his family? Didn't he care? Here were his children being taken care of by loving people and he was busy gadding off abroad on holidays.

Thankfully, my initial stay in hospital was short and I was relieved to be home but my fear of going out had turned into full-blown agoraphobia. I was now getting panic attacks even at the thought of going outside.

When I was about five months into my pregnancy, I started to bleed. Bill contacted the social worker and I was admitted until the birth of my baby. Mark, who was three by now, and Lisa, who was six, had to be fostered. They were allocated to a wonderful foster mum in Awsworth, near Kimberley. When Lisa came to visit me she was full of the adventures of the country. Mark was just happy to be with his big sister.

Once again, my baby's birth was brought forward, this time by a month. While I was in hospital, Bill was working but his income was so low that we were given family income supplement.

All the time I was in hospital I saw nothing of Stan. His so-called phobia about hospitals was a good excuse, I thought, but he did pay regular visits to the children while I was away. It was decided that a Caesarean section was the best way to deliver my baby and I soon produced another son, this time weighing just four pounds. I was relieved it was all over and it would not be long before I could go home to be with my babes.

AM I NOT A PERSON?

After I had recovered, I was wheeled to the Special Care Baby Unit and there, looking at me, was the miracle of nature. He looked like a scrag end of meat, but I could see through all the tubes and contraptions that he was a little fighter.

Despite my joy, I began to feel so angry with myself. How could I have wanted to destroy this gift from God? I was pleased that I had at least given him a chance in the world. I named my fourth child Carl David.

I was depressed because when I was sent home after nine weeks I had to leave my babe in the Special Care Unit. Meanwhile, I was told that the 'premature' nurse would be visiting my home to tell me what was best for him, so I set the carrycot up and had a thermometer hanging on it. The house was a warm, cosy place and smoking was banned.

The nurse arrived and told me that I couldn't use rubber pants on Carl. She also showed me how I should measure his milk. Then she passed the house for his arrival home.

I was happy to have my family back together. My little children had been away from home through no fault of their own and I blamed Stan for this because he would not face up to his responsibilities. I also blamed myself for not being able to sort my home situation out.

After Carl had been home some weeks, he began to develop lovely dark, curly hair in contrast to Mark's nearly white, straight hair. Carl and Lisa had little bits of putty for noses but Mark's nose was different. Stan started to question whether he really was the father of Mark, which hurt me deeply.

Not only had this man manipulated me all these years but now he was questioning me over Mark. Did he really think I was having sex with Bill? I was beside myself.

I shouldn't have to argue over my babes. Stan had been the only man I thought I loved and here he was now asking me over and over: "Am I Mark's father?"

"I'll have a blood test done to prove you are," I would yell at him, but it was just tearing me apart. Who could I turn to? This man was causing me more and more pain.

Bill was the provider, working hard and handing his wages over to keep somebody else's children. He was doing his best and I think he really cared in his own way. It wasn't his fault that I loved another man.

But Stan's commitment was non-existent and the strain of

constantly arguing with him about my double life and my existence with Bill was taking its toll.

From this moment on, my eating went completely out of control and every waking day was a nightmare. I was also mutilating my body again so that Stan could not abuse me any longer. I had started to put so much Dettol in my bath to cleanse my body that I made my vagina red raw and then I would scratch and scratch it until it bled.

I didn't want this sexual abuse to carry on and the pain was destroying me both mentally and physically. Because of my worsening agoraphobia, Lisa, who was now nine years old, had to push her two brothers to nursery and pick them up. It was such a responsibility for her. We were on the poverty line but I couldn't go out to work like normal mums did and get us out of the mess we were in.

Every health visitor I came into contact with mentioned my weight but as soon as they disappeared I would stuff myself with half a loaf and a pound of sausages. I had three young children who needed me constantly and I would read, play and sing nursery rhymes to them. I catered for their every whim. But one day, I cracked.

Stan had come around to see me but I was just sitting there, in some sort of trance-like state. The children were oblivious to this and were playing happily with their toys.

"Sylv, Sylv," he said over and over, trying to get me to recognise him, but it was no use. He knew that there was something wrong with me so he fetched the doctor and in no time at all I was admitted to St Ann's psychiatric hospital.

Apparently, I had had a total nervous breakdown. It was decided that I needed a complete rest and that is what I got. I was asleep for a week, during which time my children were once again in the care of foster parents. At least they were all together. The social worker who was assigned to the family was very caring in her placements of my children.

I was not allowed visitors but for a while seeing other people was the last thing on my mind. After my long sleep, I was allowed to wander freely but I when I looked in the mirror, I really did not like what I saw. I looked so much like Dad that I hated myself. I just went to pieces. I was given some drugs to calm me down and eventually taken to see my psychiatrist.

"Right, Sylvia," he said. "How do you feel?"

AM I NOT A PERSON?

I started to cry. This man, looking over his half-moon spectacles, was delving into my fragile emotions.

"Angry," I sobbed. As I cried uncontrollably, he could not have realised in his wildest dreams the terrible past that I had buried inside of me.

"You are very depressed, Sylvia, but I think you will feel a little better soon. I don't think your obesity helps you, but we will sort this depression out for you first."

I didn't tell him about my stay in Aston as a teenager. That part of my life was too painful. However, I have since found out that this information followed me around as part of my records. So every medical person who came into contact with me saw this and knew the label that I had been given while in Aston.

Chapter 13

The shock of ECT

What do they know?
For 40 years my secret was kept.
So many professionals saw me distraught.
"She's obese plus plus," they wrote.
These so-called professionals, inept.

After many weeks in St Ann's, it was decided that electro-convulsive therapy would help me. In their opinion, I was suffering from a personality disorder, but the only disorder I had was intense, deep-rooted anger and the unbearable pain of the past.

I was told by my doctor that he had treated many patients with ECT and it had made new people of them. But I was worried. Nobody told me what the procedure was. All I knew was that the patients having this treatment were not allowed anything to eat or drink.

I was petrified at the thought of anyone messing about with my brain. But I had no say in it because I had been sectioned. So whatever they gave me I had to endure.

I told the nurse of my fears as she prepared me but she just said: "Nothing to worry about at all, Sylvia."

The thought of these people treating me like this made me seethe with anger. I began to think that they were taking liberties of the worst kind. All the ECT patients were assembled into one room to await the treatment.

"I'm not having it," I said and walked towards the loo. But a nurse came up to me.

"Look, Sylvia, you won't know anything about it."

Then she led me back and I soon heard the porter's voice telling me to get on the trolley.

"Lay down, Sylvia."

I had built up a friendly relationship with this porter. He had seen me when I was unable to talk properly because of my drugs and he would always pass the time of day with me. He wheeled me into the ECT room and I was so frightened by what

AM I NOT A PERSON?

I saw. There, lying on the table, were electrodes to be put on my temples and switched on to give my brain a massive electric shock. My teeth started to chatter just at the thought of it. I was laid down and when I looked to the ceiling I saw a doctor above my head waiting to administer the shock.

I was given an injection before the electrodes were put on to put me to sleep. When I awoke, I found I had urinated in the bed. I didn't know where I was or even who I was.

The nurse came to me to give me a drink and I started to cry again. She told me I would be all right. After I'd had the drink I started to get my bearings but the memories of the past just came flooding back. The abuse, the rejection, they were all so vivid. The ironic thing was that I couldn't remember my children or their names for several hours, yet I could remember the painful parts of my life so clearly. I told the nurse I was not going to have any more of these treatments.

"Oh, but you have to have a course," she said to my horror.

Eventually, I was released to go home because I had finished the course. Another social worker was assigned to my family and in every report she wrote she referred to my size.

All I wanted was an arm to reach out to unburden me of the poisons in my body and mind that were destroying me … my total fear of open spaces, my inability to even open the door.

The social worker was amazed at how ill I was. She recommended a move for me and even wrote to the council.

I had to attend St Ann's regularly and on one of my visits told the doctor that I couldn't cope with open spaces. In his notes about me, I was later to find out, he said he thought I was manipulating a move by saying I had agoraphobia.

So many times these professional people had let me down. Why didn't anyone recognise that I was a survivor of sexual abuse? I was constantly splashing bleach on me and overdosing and this was merely taken as attention seeking. I needed someone to talk to, someone to relate to.

After a while, the family was on the move again to a brand new home, this time on Top Valley council estate, near Rise Park. I had made arrangements for my social worker to pick me up to take me there.

It was lovely, with a big bathroom and central heating. But in my mind, nothing would make me happy because I was married to someone I didn't love and the father of my children was living elsewhere. Our moving date arrived and my social worker helped with the removals. She even made tea for us.

I had been at Top Valley a few months when I went to my doctor and told him that I felt a complete prisoner in my own house, that my agoraphobia was so bad that I kept having panic attacks. He decided to alter my medication. To say that I became a walking zombie would be an understatement.

Chapter 14

Self-inflicted wounds

What is anger? I say.
Is it broken barbed wire to slash my wrists?
To cleanse my body of the filth and shame?
Is it shouting at loved ones to relieve the pain?
Is it wanting to jump from the highest bridge?
Is anger not wanting to live?
Is anger drinking bleach, eating soap powder to say:
"Please, please, take this filth away."?

After a few weeks, my bouts of self-hate became worse and I was slashing my wrists and overdosing. I was tormented constantly by the haunting eyes of my abusers and I simply could not cope with the pain.

On the other hand, my children knew nothing of my inner torment. I used to care for them as well as I could, airing their clothes and making their breakfast. I even managed to struggle to pay for Lisa for an exchange trip to Germany.

But one night, I just flipped. Bill had been on one of his boozing sessions and had spent most of his money and my housekeeping. He came home at about 11.00pm and I was so angry that I chased him up the road with an ornamental sword.

Somebody 'phoned the police and I was taken to hospital, sectioned again. Bill was left to take care of the children and we were assigned another social worker who I felt took an instant dislike to me. I was told that she was not happy with the home environment.

In fact, just about every social worker that was assigned to me had me admitted to hospital. In all, I was sectioned under the Mental Health Act 27 times and Mapperley Hospital became my second home.

Whenever I was in hospital, I hated myself and my body intensely. I needed to cleanse the filth. My life had been a constant battle, both emotionally and physically, and there was nothing left for me to live for. I was once again being given drugs against my will and there didn't seem to be one bit of happiness to look forward to. Were people ever going to realise that my so-called bouts of depression were bouts of self-hate? Hate for the filth floating about in my body and mind.

Was I really a depressive? I wanted to write on my forehead "I AM A SURVIVOR" because nobody seemed to understand. The system just went on abusing me, time and time again. My screams were simply silenced with drugs and more drugs, most of which were hypnotic. And although they would quell my feelings of hate for a while, when I awoke the filth and the shame were still there. I had to wash them away. I had to.

On one of my many admissions, once again doped up on a cocktail of drugs, I tried to move my body but it wouldn't go any faster than a snail's pace.

"Come on, love," the nurse said. "Let's put you to bed, you need to rest."

I had heard this over and over again every time I was incarcerated.

"I don't want to," I said in a slurred voice. It was my way of trying to be difficult, of making a stand. I was angry that I was constantly being sectioned based on hearsay. Whatever drugs they wanted to give me they could and I couldn't do a thing about it. Was I in Britain, this free country, or Communist Russia? I felt like a prisoner.

I did eventually lay down and was soon asleep, but the problem for me was when I awoke. Their eyes, their piercing eyes from the past, were always there to haunt me.

I couldn't talk about my pain to anyone. So I would simply turn both the taps on in the bathroom to see which one had the faster flowing water. To my mind's eye, the faster the flow of water the quicker the filth would be in the gutter where it belonged.

I sat on the toilet with the tap running and slashed my wrists. I felt no physical pain at all, just relief as I watched the blood, my life's blood, flowing down the drain.

Then I heard movement. I had been missed but I didn't want to be found. Why should I? It was my body and I was cleansing it. Then the nurse jumped the door.

"Oh, Sylvia."

I just stared into the distance not flinching or moving.

"Sylvia, what have you done this for?"

I looked straight ahead as if I had been struck dumb. I could feel the anger, filth, and shame just flowing out. I didn't have to talk.

"This won't solve anything, will it Sylvia? Attention seeking again ..."

This got a reaction. "I'm not, I'm not!" I yelled. "Just leave me alone!"

By this time, the charge nurse had come with dressings to see to my wounds, but the emotional pain was far worse. I couldn't tell anyone, the piercing eyes convinced me of that. No-one could ever imagine the amount of pain I had been through physically and emotionally.

Once again, I was returned to the ward but within a week I was making my way to the toilets to do it all over again. I was having constant flashbacks of the rapes and I couldn't stand it. I felt worthless.

A bag was concealed in my pocket on one trip to the toilets. This time, I would succeed. But if only I had someone to talk to. If only these professionals had recognised that I was a survivor. Just as I got to the loo, someone touched my shoulder.

"Come on Sylvia, love," a voice said. "You are not allowed to wander."

"Don't you talk to me as if I am remedial," I said, not caring if I'd used the right word.

"Sylvia, we are here to help you."

"Don't you mean drug me up? Don't think that will stop me from dying. I want to die!" I screamed.

"Go and lie down on your bed, Sylvia. You look very tired."

I could feel my body swaying. It was the effect of the enormous amount of drugs given to me, and even though I desperately wanted to talk, it was so hard. It hurt too much.

The doctor was sent for.

"How do you feel, Sylvia?" Why did they always start with that question? I ignored it anyway and burst out crying.

"Why did you stop me?"

"Stop what?"

"You've stopped me."

I couldn't say anymore. I didn't want them to know that at every opportunity I would try to cleanse my body. I felt so dirty. My life had been ruined for so long by these invaders of my body.

I can remember so vividly trying to hang myself. I was

standing on a box and had made a noose out of tights. I desperately wanted to vacate the dark tunnel of abuse.

When I pushed the box away, I could feel the noose getting tighter and tighter. My eyes were fading and suddenly, for one clear moment, I knew that I didn't want to die. I pulled feverishly at the noose and released myself. They found me with burn marks on my neck, told me I was attention seeking again, then gave me some more drugs.

Why wasn't the system recognising the signs of a survivor of sexual abuse and trying to help me, instead of labelling me a depressive and pumping me full of drugs?

Chapter 15

Madness in Mapperley?

Social workers, doctors never listened to my call
My call of anger, my call of shame.
These professionals carted me off again,
They locked me up, they gave me drugs.
I class them as brutal thugs.

I grew to hate Bill. I couldn't believe this man had a hold over me and could alter my life with just a 'phone call. Even when I was trying to hide my pain by playing records he would 'phone the hospital. I don't know why to this day, but if I was playing my country and western music this would be a cue for Bill to call Mapperley. I can only guess that he thought I was going to have some kind of turn.

On other times, I would be doing my crosswords, sometimes into the early hours when I felt at peace and the children were asleep. I found music and crosswords very relaxing and they helped me to feel something like a normal person.

However, this behaviour didn't seem normal to Bill and he would soon be down the road at the call box, telling the hospital I had 'gone' again. Before I knew it, the ambulance would pull up, Bill would let them in and I would be restrained then carted off to Mapperley Hospital. It seemed like a weekly occurrence.

Whenever this happened, my anger would boil over. I was so angry that my life and my destiny were in the hands of yet another man. The problem was that it was his word against mine, and who were they going to believe? After all, I had been labelled sub-normal from the age of 16 and I was in hospital more times than someone with a sick relative.

I would put up a real fight to try to stop the ambulance men taking me to Mapperley again. "What right have you to do this to me?!" I would scream.

I remember so vividly one occasion when Bill 'phoned the Social Services and told them that I was in a depressive state. Once again, my own voice went unheard.

AM I NOT A PERSON?

Shortly after Bill's 'phone call, a social worker arrived to assess the situation. But how could this individual manage to do this by such a cursory visit? She came in, briefcase in hand, and sat down with her notepad and pen. I could see her eyes scanning the place.

Our house was sparsely furnished but clean, although the kids' toys were all over the floor. I used to enjoy sitting for hours with them reading and playing Scrabble. The social worker started to grill me, trying to delve into the Pandora's box of my emotions and my frame of mind.

"How do you feel, Sylvia?" she began, just like all the others.

"I feel like killing the idiot," I replied without thinking, pure rage blurring my thoughts.

"Kill who, Sylvia?" she continued in that patronising voice.

"Kill Bill and everyone else," I said.

I realised as soon as I had spoken the words that I had sealed my own fate with that meaningless threat. The social worker left and I waited, expecting the worst ... but even then I was still surprised by what happened.

At around 2.00am, there was a loud bang on the back door. I slowly went towards it, fear gripping me like a vice, wondering who it was this time.

Gradually, my eyes began to adjust as I stood at the door peering into the blackness. From the shadows I made out a policewoman's face and several others standing behind her. Before I could question the policewoman, she had swept past me and up the stairs. She woke Lisa and, while the poor girl was half asleep, asked her to pack some clothes for her and the boys.

It was absolute mayhem.

Lisa was asking what was going on and the boys were crying. In fact, Mark was screaming. I became hysterical. I was hurting so badly in my body and mind and I would scream so loud because I wanted my voice to be heard ... but no-one was listening. I was led out of the house hand-cuffed and scream-ing: "What have you done to my children, you bastards?! You have no right to take them!"

I found out much later that my babes had been separated and taken to foster homes. What had I done to deserve this kind of treatment? I screamed and blurted out a constant stream of questions, not really giving anyone a chance to answer. There was a lot of activity from the people around me because I was really resisting the hand-cuffs. I was escorted to the hospital ward, still hand-cuffed and sobbing, and the ward sister came to greet me, talking to me as if I was senile.

"What has brought you here then, Sylvia?" she asked, surely not seriously expecting a reply.

I couldn't answer anyway because I didn't even know myself why I had been brought to Mapperley yet again. Was it my gaffe with the social worker? Or maybe Bill had made another call ...

Much to my relief, my hand-cuffs were released but my hands were red raw through trying to get free. I was then shown into a very basic side room which oozed coldness. There was no warmth at all, just a bed and a sad-looking quilt.

As I sat on the bed, the sister came in and asked me to put on a night-dress. It was so hard - I assumed with starch - that I wondered whether to complain about it. But I couldn't say anything, I just cried continuously. The sister told me that I had to get undressed because the doctor would soon be coming to see me.

When the doctor finally arrived, he greeted me with a smile that was meant to reassure me and asked in the same tone as the Sister: "What triggered it off this time, Sylvia?"

"That prat," I said through my tears, not knowing who to blame. "He's been making his calls again." But I wasn't interested in talking about Bill ... I had more important things on my mind. "Where are my children?" I sobbed.

I kept thinking how they must have been going through terrible pain. It must have been awful for them, watching their mother hand-cuffed and dragged out of the house in a hysterical state. Even so, I can remember so vividly Mark's piercing screams for his comfort cushion. The doctor told me that my children were all right, but that was simply not true.

"All right?!" I screamed. "How can they be all right when they are away from me?"

I was so angry - angry with my home situation, angry with the doctors and staff, and angry with the social worker who I thought must have played a major part in this episode.

The doctor told me he wanted to concentrate on making me better but I told him that I was *not* ill. Needless to say, he didn't listen.

AM I NOT A PERSON?

"How do you feel, Sylvia?" he asked [by now, I was getting fed up of hearing this same question. Do these people go through training to learn how to ask this?]. "If you tell me I can help you," he continued.

"Feel?!" I yelled back at him as I stamped my feet. "What do you think? Angry, very angry! How do you expect me to feel? I'm treated like some nutcase, dragged out of my own home in the middle of the morning and separated from my family and you ask me how I feel!?"

All I wanted to do was to get back to some sort of normality with my lovely children, but the doctor - in his wisdom - had decided that I needed some rest.

I knew what I wanted. I wanted my life back. I had been through hell in my childhood and I was fast losing control of my adult life.

After the doctor had gone, I was taken to the side room while my drugs were prepared. I tried to stand with my back to wall. I didn't want the nursing staff to see that the night-dress they had given me would not meet at the back and that my underwear was gaping out.

Not for the first time in my life, I felt so terribly alone. I didn't know where my children had gone and I had no way of finding out. And where the hell was Stan?

Just then, my mind was brought back into the here and now. I saw two nurses coming towards me and I was determined I was not going to take their evil cocktail of drugs. I knocked it out of their hands and screamed: "I'm not having it!"

Before I knew it, I was made to sit at a table while my mattress was laid on the floor. I was then dragged back into the side room and told: "Lie down, Sylvia, we're going to give you this injection."

"I don't want it!" I screamed out but, once again, I was silenced. I was held down with my arms above my head and my legs were gripped firmly by other staff. Before I had time to think, I was asleep.

[Editor's note: Within one 24-hour period, Sylvia was given the following quantities of drugs: 2200mg Sodium Amytal and 200mg Amitriptyline. On another day, she was given 400mg Chlorpromazine and 100mg Amitriptyline. Over yet another 24 hours, she was given 40mg Haloperidol, 1200mg Sodium Barbitone, 500mg Sodium Amylobarbitone and 100mg Chlorpromazine. Chlorpromazine is a neuroleptic or tranquilliser which was given at the time

AM I NOT A PERSON?

to treat severe psychoses, manic or hypomanic phases of manic depressive psychosis, affective disorders, tensions and agitation. Among its known side effects were drowsiness, skin rashes, hypotension, Parkinsonism, nightmares and blurred vision. Haloperidol, another tranquilliser, was seen as treatment for hyperactive psychotic states, mania, anxiety neuroses and behaviour disorders. Side effects included dysfunction, depression, excessive salivation and pallor. Amitriptyline was an anti-depressant meant to handle all forms of depression, anxiety, tension and psychosomatic disorders. Again, side effects included drowsiness and blurred vision with the added bonus of cardiac irregularities. Also, the drug was thought to reverse the effects of some anti-hypertensive drugs]

When I eventually came round, I was pulling at the mattress and a nurse was sitting at my side. She told me to take my time and to wake up slowly, but there was little chance of me doing that. I was semi-conscious and my head was still floating.

Seeing my condition, the soothing voice then said: "Relax, love, go back to sleep."

After an hour or so, I started to drift back into the real world but my head was still heavy. After I was helped to wash, the doctor came in to see me and asked me again how I was feeling.

"Sleepy," I said, without a hint of sarcasm.

I had been asleep for so long that my body simply did not want to wake up. Then I was given some soup. My hands were so unsteady that the nurse had to spoon feed me.

I started to cry. I wanted to see my children. How must they be feeling, being left with people they didn't know? But my clear thoughts were brief because I was given more drugs and was soon fast asleep again.

Stan later told me that he had made enquiries about me and had been told that I was 'comfortable'. He said he was also told that there were no visits allowed because I was resting.

But I did get a visit from my dear Aunt who I saw walking towards me while the nursing staff tried to hold me up. Even my legs wouldn't function properly. I was led to a table and chair and literally propped up. Aunty tried to make conversation but my only responses were "Yes" and "No".

I wasn't much company and I continually asked when I could see my social worker. If I could make contact with her, I might find out where my children were and how long it would be before we would be reunited.

Finally, my social worker arrived, and with a surprise visitor. It was Mark. I was pleased to see him but also horrified because he was covered in bruises from head to foot. He told me it was a "horrid lady" and I demanded that he be moved in with Lisa and Carl. [I was later to find out that these foster parents had been taken off the fostering list]. My bottom lip trembled as I looked at him and I started to sob:

"I want to see my children. I can't live without them."

But I had been banned indefinitely from seeing them and there was going to be a court case to obtain a care order until they were 18 years old.

Eventually, I was released from hospital and went home to an empty house. The toys were piled up but there were no children to play with them. In the hallway was Mark's cold cushion. How he must have needed that when he was in 'care'.

My first task was to tell Bill that he had to go, but that didn't take much doing. A couple of days later, when he had been on one of his boozing sessions, I got hold of him and told him that this farce had to end. We argued and I ended up putting his head through the door. Not long after that, I filed for a divorce.

I knew I'd made the right decision, even though Bill and Stan then became rivals. I just couldn't take another minute of it. The next thing was to give Stan 48 hours to move in or else I would take him to court for maintenance of the children. Lo and behold, he moved in. So far, so good. But my next task was to fight the biggest battle of my life - to get my children back.

Chapter 16

The battle for the babes

The biggest battle begins today
To try to get my babes home to stay.
Fabricated lies written about me.
All I want is for us all to be free.
To live as one happy family.

Shortly after I was released from hospital, my social worker paid me a visit. I questioned her time and time again about when I would get my children back. But she was very evasive and kept reminding me that she wanted to make sure I was well enough to cope with three noisy children.

I didn't know what she meant. I had always coped, even in the depths of despair. My children always came first. But I had difficulty coping with the sorry excuse I had for a life. The children were the only reason I carried on.

I knew that everything I did would be monitored and that any type of bad behaviour would decide my children's fate. By bad behaviour, they meant showing signs of anger, and knowing this in itself made me angry.

I had been out of hospital for some time and I still didn't know where my children were. I didn't even know if they knew that I was at home. Stan was to become my salvation when he arrived home from work.

I burst out crying: "Stan, what's happened to the children? Why can't I see them?"

Stan couldn't believe that I had been left in the dark. Then he dropped a bombshell. He told me the children had been made Wards of Court and that I wasn't to have any contact with them.

Stan had been allowed to see them and I asked him if they had been crying for me.

"Look, Sylv, they're being well looked after," was all he would say.

I was being denied the only reason I had to live. When another meeting was due with the social worker, Stan told me we must be seen to be all 'lovey dovey' [at most meetings, we would end up arguing].

"They will have no excuse for the children not coming home," he said. "You see, Sylv, what they are doing is getting us upset and that way they can say our relationship is unstable."

"Stan, I can't live without them. Why am I being punished in this way? Surely they must realise that I would do anything for my children? You know I wouldn't harm them."

Stan started to explain to me what had happened to them the night they were dragged into care. He told me Lisa and Carl had been placed in a children's home in Sherwood, five minutes from the Nottingham city centre. Great, I thought, I've got a lead. I would be able to trace two of my children.

But when Stan continued with his tale, I realised that they had all been moved around over the last few weeks. Then he told me that all three of them had eventually landed up in a foster home.

By this time, we had been separated for five weeks and Stan could see the desperation in my face. He spoke to me in a reassuring voice.

"Look, ducky, the foster mother who is caring for the children is appalled by the way you have been treated. She doesn't agree with you not having contact with your kids. She says she knows of children that have been ill-treated and their parents are allowed to visit, to even take them out sometimes."

He surprised me when he added: "She gave me this number, Sylv, for you to phone her. Hopefully, you will be able to talk to the children and they will be able to hear their Mummy."

He grabbed my hand as the tears started to flow.

"What are they going through Stan?" I asked, then I snatched the 'phone number from him without waiting for a reply. Stan went out and I dialled the number, my hands trembling. I wanted to be strong. I am not going to cry, I told myself, but I didn't know how the children would react. Would they blame me for our separation? Would they understand why we had been parted?

The 'phone rang and rang. Please answer, please be in. Then ...

"Hello," a very soft spoken woman said on the other end.

"Um, hello, this is Lisa, Mark and Carl's Mum. I hope you

don't mind me calling but I really need to know how the children are."

"Hello, love, my name's June. Of course I don't mind you calling. I'm glad you have. I believe you should be allowed to see your children and I am pressurising the social worker to organise it. I will probably get into trouble but it's a little bit late to worry about that."

She sounded so jolly.

I appreciated the fact that this lady understood how a mother felt. Half the social workers I have dealt with have never been around children, so how on earth could they relate to how I was feeling? However, I was unable to speak to my babes on this occasion. They were out playing.

I desperately wanted to talk to them but June suggested something far better. She was going to allow me to visit them. I was overjoyed. We arranged a time at the weekend and I began to count the days before I would see my babes. I kept myself busy decorating Lisa's bedroom in her favourite colour, lilac, and carpeting the boys' room. Although I was busy, the week dragged on.

I had bought the children little bits and bobs, sweeties and things, even though my purse strings were stretched to the limit. I packed Mark's cold cushion in my bag and Stan promised to take me. As we drove through the country lanes, I thought again how wonderful Mother Nature was. I was sure the children must have loved the change, coming from the city centre to this.

When I arrived, I couldn't get over the size of the house. It was detached and in the middle of a beautiful rural setting, totally different to the small townhouse the children were used to. I opened the gate and my heart was pounding. Aching too, because I questioned why I should be doing this. My babes should be at home with me.

Lisa was first out of the door to greet me. She ran up to me and gave me an almighty hug. I picked her up and just kissed her over and over.

"Hello, darling," I eventually said. Her glasses were steamed up with tears.

"Mum, I hate this school," she said in between sobs. "The lads keep calling me 'four eyes' and 'gypsy'. They say I haven't got a real home."

AM I NOT A PERSON?

Children can be so cruel. My eyes were filled with tears. As if Lisa hadn't enough to cope with emotionally, she had to contend with name calling. Carl was nowhere in sight. He had always been an outdoor lad and he was fishing somewhere. He was a carefree soul, but I knew I would see him later.

Before Mark appeared, Lisa continued with her news. "You wouldn't believe it Mum, but when Mark came to us he was covered in bruises."

Lisa didn't know I had demanded from my hospital bed that he be moved in with her and Carl.

We walked into the house but before I could say anything to June, Lisa stunned me with her next words.

"That social worker," she said, "she keeps taking us on walks and saying you have done horrible things to us. She keeps asking if you ever hit us."

I knew the social services were trying to get a care order on my children and that they needed as much evidence as they could get, but I never thought that individuals would stoop so low as to put words into my children's mouths.

June, the foster mum, was busying herself so I could have some time on my own with my children. I didn't want it to end but when she came back into the room, I thanked her from the bottom of my heart for caring for them. She was a wonderful person and so generous.

"Anytime, Sylvia," she said with a smile. "Come and see the children again. Just give me a ring."

When I got to see Mark, he was very weepy and a little bit distant. The ill treatment and being away from home had obviously left a scar on him. Carl was totally different. He was all smiles and told me he had been bird watching using binoculars that I had bought him. Carl asked when he was coming home but was full of the adventures he had been on. He was being kept active and that made him happy.

I was very worried about Mark and I asked June how he had been when he arrived. She told me that apart from the bruises, he was very quiet and a loner. Mark had a fear of dogs and with the other foster family he had been shut up in a room with a few boys. If he tried to open the door he was met by an Alsatian dog that had been fastened to the door handle. No wonder the poor lad had become withdrawn.

To this day, Mark, now a strapping 6' 3" lad in his twenties, does not speak to me about his ordeal. He has told his girlfriend and that is where it ends for him.

My time with the children seemed to fly by on this visit. Lisa was clinging to me like glue. Mark was busy undoing his little present while Carl had gone outside again, looking for worms. It was soon time to leave and I kept wondering what was going on in my children's minds. Were they blaming me? As I put Lisa on my knee, instinct told her I was about to say goodbye and she looked sad. I knew I had to be strong.

"I'm going to have to go now. It won't be long before you're home for good."

"Mum, you're not leaving me ..." She was sobbing.

She fetched Mark and Carl and they linked arms around me so I could not leave. I was heartbroken. Why should my babes endure this mental cruelty? When Lisa let go to dry her eyes, I started to make towards the door. June got hold of Lisa's hand and gave her a reassuring cuddle.

As I walked to Stan's car, I turned around and through my tear-stained glasses saw that Lisa was absolutely hysterical. I blew her a kiss and got into the car.

While he drove along, I asked him: "Why have the children got to go through this?"

But there was a silence, broken only by my sobs.

The children had been in care for about seven weeks and I was still no nearer to getting them back. But there was a senior social worker I had faith in who also trusted me and was trying to make life that little bit easier. The neighbours also got a petition together, demanding that my children be returned to me. They all knew I was devoted to them.

The kind social worker had seen the pain on my children's faces and knew that they loved me. She had even checked the school out to ascertain whether there were any problems with their school work. She was told that my children were academically good, especially Lisa who was a model pupil.

Today, I reflect and ask: "Do these sound like abandoned and unloved children?"

The social worker told me she was trying to arrange for my children to come home for the weekend. I was so excited. I wanted to do everything right. Before the day arrived, I put all their favourite toys out and rigged up Carl's computer. Once again it looked like a home of happiness. I wanted the social worker to see the real me, the woman who adored her children. I wanted her to see that they had no right keeping us apart.

The afternoon I knew they were coming, I made Carl his favourite chocolate Instant Whip. I also made Mark bananas and custard which he adored and made Lisa her favourite flapjacks. I had laid out everything, scones, crisps and nuts, for their 'homecoming'. I had even made ice cream milk shakes.

Then I heard the car pull up. I looked out of the window and saw Mark with his lovely blond hair flying back as he raced to the back door. Carl was following and Lisa was already looking for me. I opened the door and they all clambered around me, kissing and hugging me. They were full of chatter.

When Lisa saw her bedroom, she said: "Mum, this is lovely."

Mark and Carl ran into their room and jumped on to their bunk beds. Then they shot downstairs and looked in every room before asking if they could go to see Jay, their best mate.

"Of course, ducky."

The social worker left and told me a precise time when she would be back. I don't think the boys realised that they would have to go back to the children's home but Lisa did. She told me secretly that she was not going back with the social worker.

"When she comes, I'm going to lock myself in the bathroom. If she wants me she will have to knock the door down."

Were these the words of a child who had been ill-treated by her mother? I put my arm around her and said: "Look Lisa, you will have to go back. You will make it worse for yourself and Mummy if you don't."

Once again she started to cry: "But, Mum ..."

"I know how upset you are Lisa, but if you play up they might not let you come home again. It's just this once, love. You will be back home soon for good, I promise."

I just hoped in my heart that I could keep that promise. I knew the social worker would be arriving in another 15 minutes and I was dreading it. Mark and Carl had come back and were playing with their games while Lisa was stuck to me like glue. When the social worker turned up, the atmosphere was very tense and Lisa had indeed disappeared into the bathroom. The social worker told the boys that they would be home soon if they were good today. She then coaxed Lisa out and I kissed them all before they were taken away.

AM I NOT A PERSON?

Even though I was grateful to the social worker for her efforts, I said to her before she left: "Do you realise what this is doing to my children? They are going through mental torture."

The neighbours' petition was now in the hands of a solicitor and their actions had confirmed that I was a good mother. They knew my kids were well cared for and that if anyone ever went without, it was usually me.

My children had been to hell and back and I was determined to put my case to the courts. They had undergone a medical which meant having to strip naked and be examined thoroughly. Lisa was extremely embarrassed. She was nine years old and her body was becoming more personal to her everyday and now she was asked to lay naked in front of total strangers. Wasn't this abuse of my children? Incidentally, I never did ascertain what the point of this medical was.

Then, like a bolt from the blue, three days after the children's weekend visit, I received a 'phone call. It was the senior social worker. She told me that she had cancelled the interim care order so the children could come home until the court hearing. But she stressed that for the next few weeks, the whole family would be under the watchful eye of the social services.

I had to win this case. I had several meetings with my solicitor and just the thought of losing my children still haunts me today. I had them back home but every time I looked at them I wondered how long it would last. What if the court case went against me? What if the judge believed the unfavourable reports written by the other social worker? What if ...?

My solicitor was very confident that the verdict would go in my favour. He had taken details of my house and said that it was big enough for all of us, it was clean and there was always plenty of food. All I could do now was pray.

During those few weeks waiting for the court date, I didn't dare raise my voice at the children. I was scared that even chastising them might go against me, so they were kept on a very loose rein.

As the day drew ever closer, I became a bag of nerves. I was so out of control with my eating and was consuming anything and everything. So much hinged on the way that my case was put across and I hated the fact that I was leaving the fate of my life and my children's in the hands of virtual strangers. But that's the system and I had to trust it.

AM I NOT A PERSON?

I considered the case put forward on behalf of the social services to be pure fabrication. They accused me of scalding Mark with boiling water and holding him for a long time in front of the fire. I was absolutely astonished that they could even think such a thing. Mark had never been taken to the hospital or doctors with any injuries and they simply had no proof of such treatment.

My defence put forward a different story. Would children that were being poorly treated want to go back home? Would they want to stay in a place where they were not safe? These were rhetorical questions but they hit home and they finally paid off.

I was absolutely elated when the judge gave his verdict. He said the whole thing should never have been brought to court and there was no case to answer. The children would not be placed under a supervision order. They would be allowed to stay with me.

Life could now get back to some sort of normality and I hoped that this farce would not affect my children for the rest of their lives.

However, they had been placed on an 'at risk' register by the social services, so a social worker would still call periodically, which affected the way I brought my children up. So much so that I became unable to chastise them in case 'Big Brother' was watching. I was totally soft with them and, more often than not, they used this to their advantage. I can't say they were spoiled, my finances wouldn't permit that, but they never wanted for anything within my reach.

It was heaven to me to see the children playing football with Stan. It should have happened years ago.

My criticism is not of the social services itself but of one individual social worker who nearly lost me my children forever. However, this is countered by my gratitude for the other social worker who played a major part in getting them back.

Chapter 17

Getting out

The flashbacks are still coming,
Their eyes, their smells are there every waking day.
It's hell.

Even though my agoraphobia was so bad that the thought of just waving the children goodbye at the door gave me terrible shakes, they wanted me to be like any other mother. I remember so vividly Carl running in when he was about six saying:

"Mum, Mum, will you take us to Bulwell bogs to catch some tiddlers?"

"I can't, babe, I can't," I said and his big, blue eyes filled with tears. His little adventure had been stopped through my fear of open spaces and it made me feel bad.

I became more and more reliant on my friend who would do my shopping for me because I was forever asleep. The drugs that I was still on were knocking me out and I desperately wanted to break free. I wanted to be like any other mum, to take the children out, to go for picnics. I dreamed of the day that I could do this.

One year, when it was coming up to the six weeks school summer holidays, I wanted this break to be special. I had woken one particular morning and my darling Lisa had made me a coffee. But I got out of bed immediately, repeating to myself: "This is it. This is it."

She looked at me in amazement. I went to the cupboard and collected all my pills, then went upstairs and flushed them down the loo.

Lisa only had a couple of days left at school so she decided she wanted to stay with me and do my shopping. I seemed more awake when the boys came home and was able to communicate with them.

That night I went to bed early, read then fell asleep, content that I had rid myself of those mind-numbing drugs. But the next morning I couldn't move. I was sweating, shaking and I felt

114

violently sick. My friend had arrived for a coffee as usual and it took me an age to shift out of my bed.

"Sylv," she said. "I came to see if Carl wants to come with us on an adventure."

"Oh yes, he would love that."

Not long after she left, I was in bed again.

I lay on the bed and could see spiders crawling up the wall. There were spiders all over the bed and my whole body was in some sort of spasm. I was so ill. I knew I had come off all the tranquillisers too quickly but I wanted a life.

Within a week, when the children had broken up from school, I was feeling a little stronger in my mind.

I confided in Lisa: "I'm going to tackle my agoraphobia."

Lisa looked at me in disbelief but she was very supportive. Obviously, she wanted me to go to the shops with her and she wanted me to be at school for her open nights. Also, the boys were keen for me to take them to school.

Then it finally came, the day of reckoning. I told Lisa that I was going to step outside.

"Well, Mum, you can do it, you know."

I felt quite humble, my 14-year-old daughter being so understanding. She had moved the kitchen chair to be close to the door and had made me a coffee. I sat there just thinking, my heart pounding. I was sweating like a bull.

"Right then," I said expecting Lisa to say something. But she just opened the door.

"I can't. I can't."

"You can, Mum. Come on, or else you will never do it." Then she went running to the bottom of our garden and shouted up: "Come on, Mum!"

I stepped out into the open and my feet felt like blocks of concrete. It was as if they were fixed to the ground. I felt paralysed, unable to move forward or backward. I felt naked. For one brief moment I was able to move back into the kitchen. I banged the door shut, ran into the lounge and fell on the settee sobbing.

"Mum, Mum!" Lisa called, trying to get me to come out again.

"I can't Lisa, I can't!" I yelled and that was my last step outside for three weeks.

Lisa had told me that she cared for me and that she was going to help me. "I love you, Mum, and I want you to be with me."

Those words convinced me that I had to do it. I wanted to conquer this terrible affliction. I wanted to be with Lisa and I wanted to be free.

One day, Lisa said: "Right, Mum, you're going to do it today."

Once again, I had her waiting at the bottom of the garden but just the thought of the door opening paralysed me. If I could take some deep breaths I might, just might be able to do it. I breathed in several times and could feel my heart pounding, but I stepped outside.

I could hear Lisa shouting but it felt as though she was miles away. I put my foot forward and once again felt naked. But before I knew it, I had walked three steps to the dustbin. As I leaned over it I could hear Lisa shouting: "Yes Mum, yes Mum!"

She came up to me and smothered me with kisses. I rushed back into the house and was shaking from head to foot. But I was proud of my achievement. Lisa had decided that the next day I should try to go to the newsagents across the road.

I knew that if I could just get over my agoraphobia, I would be like most mums to my lovely children.

After breakfast the next day, Lisa helped me dry the pots. She was talking to me all the time, trying in her own way to take my mind off the next fearful step for me. But when she helped me to put my cardigan on I started to panic.

"I can't, Lisa, I can't," and I ran upstairs.

"Don't you love me, Mum?" Lisa asked when she found me, "'cos if you do, you would come with me."

That little comment pulled at my heart strings and soon, the front door opened and I was taking loads of deep breaths. We walked down half a dozen steps and my legs felt like jelly. Lisa was talking to me all the time to me and I felt faint.

"Come on, you can do it, Mum. Don't let us down."

As we slowly walked I could feel my whole body swaying. Lisa put her arm in mine.

"Mum, we are nearly there."

I stepped into the paper shop and Lisa let out a cheer. She bought me some Polo mints and we walked back. I was on the way to recovery and this time around the shakes weren't so bad.

AM I NOT A PERSON?

The following morning, Lisa told me she was taking me for a ride on the bus. I wanted to do it but the fear sent me into a mega sweat. I did my deep breathing and once again we were outside.

"It's only a short way to the bus stop, Mum."

I felt ill. I hadn't been on a bus for over 10 years. As we stood at the bus stop I started to cry.

"What's the matter, Mum?"

"I feel sick."

"Now, Mum, just take some deep breaths."

Lisa got hold of my hand and squeezed it. I knew she loved me so much and I just had to do it. I got on the bus and Lisa made sure I was near the front. My mind was in a daze and I was shaking. I just jumped up and rang the bell. My mind got the better of me. While I stood waiting to get off, Lisa informed the driver that I had made a mistake. I was so cross with her, I felt that she didn't care. But I know that without her firmness I would not have been cured. We walked back home and from that day my agoraphobia was no more.

The children were proud of me and I took them out whenever funds permitted. I even went to the boys' open night and to see their faces was wonderful.

Chapter 18

Jaws

I hate men, I hate them
They destroyed my body and mind.
Please, Lord, let me find
Self-control on the food front
So society can accept me into the fold.

I was still attending the out patients of St Ann's Hospital in 1980 when the doctors there told me they thought my so-called depression was due to gross obesity. God knows, I couldn't cope with being thin but by now I weighed 24½ st [and only 5' 4" tall]. The doctor said he wanted to refer me to a specialist about my weight problem and would write to the obesity clinic at the General Hospital so I could discuss it with them. I went home and told Stan about the doctor's suggestion.

"Great Sylv, great," he said. "You will look lovely."

"I don't want to look lovely!" I snapped back.

When my appointment arrived I was very nervous. I didn't really want to go but on the other hand I now looked on my size as a disability that was causing me great discomfort.

I never wanted to be like Twiggy but I was at the stage that I could hardly move. Stan told me I must go to the clinic for the children's sake and he took me, with Connie along for support as usual. I was embarrassed and shuffled into the reception area feeling worthless and dejected.

"I'm Mrs ------," I said [which I still was, even though Bill was no longer in my life].

"Oh, sit down, please and wait for your name to be called."

I stood because I knew I would not be able to get up if I sat down for too long. My name was called after a few minutes and I was taken into the weighing room. Regretfully, I was too big and had to be taken to another building to be weighed on the parcel scales. I was screaming inside.

I shuffled back to the reception area to wait for my name to be called again, then I was led into the doctor's room.

"Right Mrs ------," he said, "you are grossly obese and this is putting a massive strain on your heart. You are at high risk of heart trouble and I must inform you that we do not do the bypass operation anymore. It is too risky."

There was silence for a second or two, then he asked me about my food intake.

"Well," I began, "for breakfast I can eat a whole loaf, a 1lb of sausages and six eggs with beans and lard. I can eat three packets of biscuits mid-morning, and a whole chicken, 5lbs of potatoes and any amount of veg for my main meal."

The doctor just looked at me with his mouth open.

"Er … well, Mrs ------, I have to congratulate you on your honesty. We have patients who come here with severe weight problems and say they don't eat very much."

He went on: "I believe that we can help you by having your jaws wired."

"What does that entail, doctor? Is it painful?"

"No, we freeze your gums. I'll demonstrate what we will do, but first we must check your teeth."

I sat in his reclining chair and he told me there were no major problems with my teeth, just the odd filling or two. When I got off the chair, he showed me the metal plates which would be cemented to my teeth.

"God!" I gasped. They resembled something out of a James Bond movie.

He told me the next stage was to take a mould of my teeth and I would have to make another appointment.

Despite the horror of seeing these metal plates, the only thing on my mind as I left the clinic was food. What were the doctors trying to do to me? To deprive me of the only solace I had would destroy me. On the way home, I told Stan:

"I'm not going through with it. Why should you or anybody else for that matter decide what my body should look like. I don't want to be thin!"

"Look, ducky, don't start getting annoyed with me. Let's go home and have a cuppa and talk about it."

"Talk about it?!" I yelled at Stan. "Are you going to feel the pain? When they fit the plates I will have five needles in my gums!"

Stan cringed and for the first time he seemed to understand something about my pain. "Yes, you wouldn't want to go through that, would you?"

AM I NOT A PERSON?

No more was said but when Lisa arrived home from school, Stan immediately told her: "Your mum's not having her jaws wired. She's too scared."

"Would you go through with it Stan?" I said, annoyed at him. "I know you bloody well wouldn't. Could you manage without your bacon and eggs?"

Connie was due 'round at any time and I knew I could confide in her. She said that she certainly wouldn't go through with it herself but that it was my decision. My food intake was in overdrive. I was eating constantly and a few days before my next appointment I had eaten a two litre tub of chocolate-flavoured ice cream. After all, I figured that once I was wired up, I wouldn't be able to have these niceties.

Stan made sure I was up on time but finding something for me to wear was a headache. I was unable by now to fit into any clothes and couldn't even put my shoes on. I knew that no man would ever love me while I was like this, so I didn't feel threatened. I sat there and told Stan: "I'm not going."

"Come on, duck, you've got to."

He was getting very annoyed with me and went to wait in the car. Before long, I shuffled over to it and climbed in.

"Right ducky," he said. "Don't worry about a thing."

We drove along for a few minutes when I shouted: "Stop! Stop! Let me get a paper to read."

He stopped at a newsagents but it wasn't a paper I was after. When I shuffled back to the car I was cramming a full packet of Rolos into my mouth. My cheeks were bulging and when I sat back in the car Stan gave me a look of disgust but didn't say anything. He had learned from past experiences not to say a word.

We arrived at the hospital and I shuffled into the toilets to rub my teeth with tissue to remove any traces of chocolate. I came back into the waiting room and not long afterwards my name was called.

"Right, Sylvia," the dentist said, "I want you to put this mould into your mouth."

It resembled Plasticine. When I put it on my teeth I felt as though I was about to throw up. I took a deep breath and gripped as hard as I could. After I had released my jaws, I was told the impression was all right.

"Now Sylvia, let's get your fillings over and done with."

AM I NOT A PERSON?

When he had sorted those out, I was given an appointment for the following week for my wiring, but I knew that I wasn't going to keep it. I came out of the building red faced and sweating and instantly yelled at Stan who was waiting outside:

"Do you know what? You are the biggest coward. Why didn't you wait in the waiting area with me?"

"I don't like hospitals, Sylv," he said again, this time adding: "Look ducky, when you have this done you will feel and look like a new woman."

In between dental appointments I had to see my doctor at St Ann's because I was still on the anti-depressants. For several days before I went, I stuffed my face with chocolates, biscuits, crisps, tuna and lots of sweet and sour things together. Stan was out and I was making up packets of instant potato with lashings of margarine followed by tins of chilli. But my luck ran out. On one of my binges, Stan walked through the door and caught me. I felt like a little girl again, full of anguish.

The following day was the jaw wiring appointment and I had a mega row with Stan. I was petrified of not being able to eat.

"Can you manage without your ciggies, Stan?"

"Sylv, that's different."

"No, Stan, it isn't."

The children were full of their usual chatter as I got ready and Lisa said: "I hope you go on all right, Mum, at the hospital."

"Thanks, ducky. I will be back home by the time you finish school."

Again, Stan drove me to the hospital and Connie came along. All too soon, it was my turn.

"How are you, Sylvia? Nervous?" the dentist enquired. "Don't worry, you won't feel a thing."

I got into the chair and as the lights beamed down I saw the dental surgeon coming towards me. The nurse carried the needles on her kidney shaped tray. I tensed my body and the dentist stuck two needles in my top gum and three in the bottom. Then I went into the waiting area until the injections took effect.

I sat talking to Connie but my tongue began to feel twice its normal size and the whole of my mouth was becoming numb. Then my name was called again and I was directed once more to the reclining chair. Before I lay back, I saw the metal clamps with a cement-like substance inside.

AM I NOT A PERSON?

"Open wide, Sylvia," said the dentist, and within seconds the clamp was pushed over my bottom teeth. The sensation of suction was something else. Then the next mould was put on my top teeth. The cement-like substance stuck and there were four hooked metal pieces protruding off the clamps. The dentist got what looked like thick fuse wire and used pliers to twist it around the hooks top and bottom so that each hook was fixed with wire.

I felt my jaw getting tighter and I my heart pounding louder. It felt so final. After a last twist with the pliers, my jaws were well and truly locked tight. But inside I was screaming. Didn't anyone understand my need for food?

Then I was told to see the dietician so that she could reinforce what I needed to take to stay healthy. I had seen her several times and she knew me quite well. She told me to drink plenty of skimmed milk, as well as Oxo, clear vegetable soup, and custard made with Sucron.

Connie was trying to make me feel better as I left the clinic and we got into Stan's car. He just looked at me and said: "Come on, duck."

"The pain, the pain," I sobbed. "My gums are throbbing." Connie sat in the back and tried to console me. She was so good to me but Stan didn't utter another word.

When I arrived home, I started to cry buckets. "Why is everybody so keen for me not to eat?"

"Your weight, Sylv."

I tried to shout back but I couldn't, my teeth were held solidly together. The children arrived home as usual and Mark asked to see my teeth. I grinned at him and he stood there speechless for the first time in his life.

I was still expected to cater for all the family's meals, which in itself was hell. While they tucked into hearty meals, I would sit with my straw and a cup of Oxo. But it was working. The weight was dropping off my body at a rapid pace, around a stone a week. I had to admit to myself that I was able to walk better and I began to fit into some of my abandoned clothes. I was craving for a slice of toast with the margarine all soaked in.

"Stan, I can't stand it," I raged. "I can't cope."

"Not much longer, ducky," he whispered.

But first we had to get through Christmas, and I knew that dishing the dinner out would be one thing that I couldn't cope with. I cooked it and Stan dished it out while I sat with my mug of turkey gravy. I was desperate, and I mean desperate. I had a notion that if I broke minute bits of turkey up I would be able to push them through the gap in my wired teeth. I even tried it but it was no good. Then I managed to liquidise some Brussels sprouts, but they weren't the same.

I started to get my figure back but I hated it so I would put bleach into my bath water. Nobody was going to have my body, and I didn't want Stan to find me sexually attractive. I also started to cut myself under the covers again. I hated the signs of my shapely body showing through. After four months I had lost in excess of 6st and my neighbours had started to pass comments like: "Is that Sylv?" My weight had reduced to an acceptable size for society and this made me so angry.

My children adored their Mum whether she was fat or thin. It was the doctors and society - and especially Stan - that could not accept me the way I was. He wanted my perfect body. Even the social worker would call and tell me how wonderful I looked.

"Do you know how I feel inside?" I would snap, but nobody did.

Because Stan was now on a lower wage bracket, I decided at this time to improve my financial status. The children were well and truly independent now, so I started to scan the paper for a job. I came across one at Tesco in the Victoria Centre in Nottingham, stacking shelves. A mundane job, but it would be a start. As I searched my wardrobe looking for something to wear, I decided even if my jaws were wired I had as much chance as anybody of getting the job and, at last, we would have a better standard of living. Life had always been a struggle and I would now, hopefully, be able to give my children a little extra.

I was being denied my only comfort and I was so desperate to take my mind off the continuing torture, so I phoned Tesco up and was pleased when a few days later I got an interview. My first job interview in over 20 years!

The day arrived and I managed to find some clothes to fit me. They weren't the best, but they were presentable. When my name was called, I was nervous. Here we go Sylv, I thought. I sat down and the personnel officer asked why I had applied for the job.

AM I NOT A PERSON?

"Well, I want to improve my financial status."

She asked me a few more questions then told me the hours and the wage structure. I was told that I would hear within the week whether my application had been successful. Throughout the interview, she looked me straight in the eye and not once at my clamp, even when I explained to her that I had been wired up to reduce my weight.

I arrived home, convinced that Stan was hoping that I wouldn't get the job. If I did, I would no longer be reliant on him financially for all of my needs. It didn't feel like very long before the 'phone rang.

"Hello, Sylvia ------," I said.

"Hello, Mrs ------, it's personnel here at Tesco. I am pleased to tell you that we can offer you a job in our store, not shelf filling but on the tills on the main bread counter two days a week."

I was thrilled. I was pleased that somebody believed in my ability to work the tills in a busy store and it would take my mind off the mental torture I was going through. But being denied food and working around it every day was going to be unbearable.

When I arrived I was asked what size I was. I told them 18 and was given three overalls and three caps.

"You must wear these at all times while at work. Put your overall and hat on and I will introduce you to the girls. I was so pleased with myself, even though I was nervous of going into the world of the unknown. I didn't know the first thing about tills but I was willing to learn.

There were shelves of hot baked bread and my taste buds went mad. My mind was working overtime - best butter, jam, honey, all these niceties that I couldn't have. I was introduced to the girls and for a second I forgot about my clamp. I gave them a smile and they all seemed to take a step back.

I was told my supervisor would train me on the tills which I began to believe had minds of their own. I did my fair share of voids in the first week. I think my supervisor was wondering if I would ever make the grade but before long I was put on the main shopping mall tills and I was proud of myself. I had achieved the impossible.

My customers on the bread counter treated me with respect and week by week I was reducing in size. That was, until I was

AM I NOT A PERSON?

left to count all the cakes for the pig bin - cream cakes, apple doughnuts, chocolate eclairs. As I stood there, I ran my finger along the cream and jam and tried to push it through the gap in my wired up jaw. I had the stuff all over my face but the bits I pushed through the gap were heaven.

I would also buy my children apple tarts and doughnuts as well as packs of damaged best butter and dented tins. Life was taking a turn for the better and the kids helped with the housework. They realised that Mum was able to hold a respectable job down and they no longer needed their school clothing vouchers and free dinners. We were on the up. Stan seemed to take a back seat for a while. He was not the main person in my life anymore. I was.

One day, I arrived home after a hard day's work and had a bath to unwind. Stan had gone to bed and I was reading until about 11.30pm. I went to bed as usual, after checking the children were covered up and cosy.

I felt so tired.

I wondered whether I was anaemic through lack of food because I had been feeling quite dizzy. After all, I had had my clamps on for six months. I dozed off to sleep, dreaming about chocolate, chocolate, and more chocolate, when I awoke with a sudden jolt. Somehow, in my sleep my wires holding my clamp together had snapped. I felt little fragments of cement in my mouth. I was free! I couldn't believe it. As I opened my jaw it clicked.

I slid out of bed, crept downstairs and ate corn flakes, corned beef, bread, soup, crisps, biscuits. I was eating until about 5.00am and when I eventually went to bed it was as if I had been anaesthetised. I was soon well and truly fast asleep.

I decided the next day that nobody was going to know that my clamp had snapped, not for a while anyway. Stan shouted me for my usual cuppa since it was the only thing I could enjoy. When I came downstairs, I had to talk as if my clamp was still in one piece, which was difficult. After seeing the children off to school, I began to get ready for work. But I looked at myself in the mirror and saw the curves of my body in all the right places. I went to pieces and started to cry. I ran into the bathroom and scratched my private parts until they bled.

On my way to the bus stop, I bought chocolate, more chocolate and crisps. As I sat on the bus, I had to check there was no-one on there that knew me before I tucked in. Once again, I was the little girl being naughty.

When I arrived at work I told my friends what had happened and they encouraged me to eat what I wanted. So, in between serving customers, I was eating jam doughnuts and any cake that came my way.

But I felt guilty deceiving Stan and the kids and I knew I could not do it for much longer. When I got home, Stan had made my usual cuppa.

"Have you had a good day, duck?"

"Yes," I replied, with my mouth open.

"What's going on, Sylv?"

"Oh, it snapped while I was at work, Stan," I lied, "and I am *not* having it redone."

When I dished everybody's dinners out I gave myself a huge mountain of instant mash with loads of butter on. Stan was furious.

"I'm telling Connie. I mean it, Sylv. You will put all your weight back on."

"That's what I want."

"I'm convinced there's something wrong with you, Sylv," he said, uncharitably.

"Yes, there is!" I screamed. "I don't want to be attractive to you or anybody. I don't want the perfect figure. I've lost too much weight. Over 10st!"

"I'm taking you back in the morning," Stan said, then there was a silence. Once again, I was being chastised.

The next day Stan was up bright and early but I was not due into work until later.

"Come on, duck."

"What's your problem, Stan?" I knew what he wanted but I was determined I wasn't going back to the dentist.

"Come on, let's get your clamp fitted."

I was so angry inside. He was manipulating me again and, yes, he did wear me down and win in the end.

The dentist looked at my clamps and could see that I had been on a mega binge.

"This won't help your weight to reduce," he said, showing a knack for stating the obvious.

"I'm not bothered," I grinned.

The dentist twisted the wires and once again I was being

denied my only comfort. What right had these people to do this to me?

Back home, the mental torture felt worse the second time around and as the weeks went by it became too much to bear. I couldn't live another day without food. I had told several people that this was causing me even more pain than being overweight but I was ignored.

Never mind, I had found a full bottle of anti-depressants and decided to end my agony. I caught a bus into town, found a place in the centre where no-one could see me and put the tablets through my gap. The next thing I remember is waking up in the General Hospital free, free of my clamps.

My nightmare had ended. Stan was furious with me but I was left alone to eat and eat as much as I liked. I wasn't given any more appointments for the obesity clinic because in their eyes I was a waste of time and effort. So I was left to my own devices of bingeing and splashing bleach over myself.

Within six months, I felt safe again. The weight had started to pile back on but it meant I was unable to work once again.

By now, Lisa was nearly ready to leave school. I was so proud of her and when I saw her dressed up it was like a mirror image of me at 16. There was to be a school disco and she had bought a new ankle length skirt from Miss Selfridges and a new blouse. She looked stunning.

Stan dropped her off with all her records which she was loaning to the DJ and said he would be back to pick her up after the disco.

"No, Dad, it's all right. Lucy is walking back with me," she replied independently.

When she came home she was pretty red but I put that down to her disco dancing. She came in, said a quick "'Night, Mum" and went straight upstairs. Soon afterwards, I locked up and went to bed. I got up bright and early the next day to see the boys off and to have a natter with Lisa. Carl had gone by 8.30. He loved his rugby and that's all he and his friends seemed to talk about. I waited for Lisa but she didn't get up. When I went upstairs to wake her, I never imagined what would happen.

I went into her bedroom and she started to sob: "The bastards, the bastards."

I sat down. "What's the matter Lis?"

AM I NOT A PERSON?

"Mum, I was assaulted last night by five boys."

"Right," I said immediately, "we're going to the police."

I didn't know what they had done but I knew they wouldn't get away with it. We arrived at the police station and an officer showed us into an interview room.

Lisa started to tell them what had happened and when she went into detail I began to shake. I was right back in that dark room with those piercing eyes and those hands all over my defenceless body. Lisa said that these boys had their hands everywhere and that she screamed. There were houses all around but nobody came out. Lucy had run off. She was scared.

"Don't worry," Lisa was told, "when we apprehend them, they will be straight inside."

The humiliation my daughter had to face, with the police asking her if she dressed provocatively. Of course Lisa didn't, but that's beside the point. No man should have the right to assault a 16-year-old or a woman of any age.

Soon after this, I bought Lisa an Alsatian puppy and we trained it to protect her. She was in the middle of her exams when the alleged attack happened, but I'm pleased to say that she passed two months later. We found out that the youths - who lived just five minutes away from our house - were released with a caution.

I wrote to the Chief Constable to see why they weren't prosecuted but it seems Lisa's friend didn't want to give a statement and there simply wasn't enough evidence.

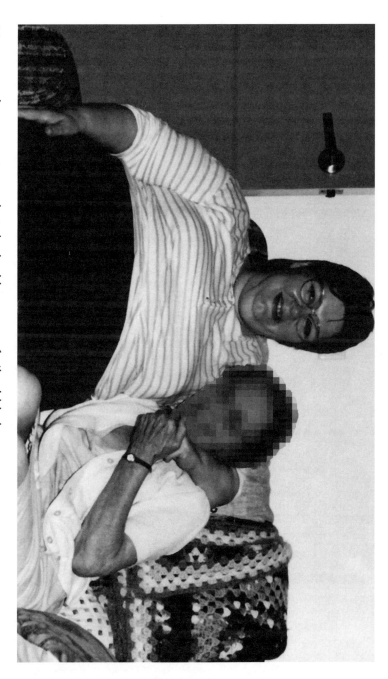

Mum was always so strong, but she had become a frail, old lady

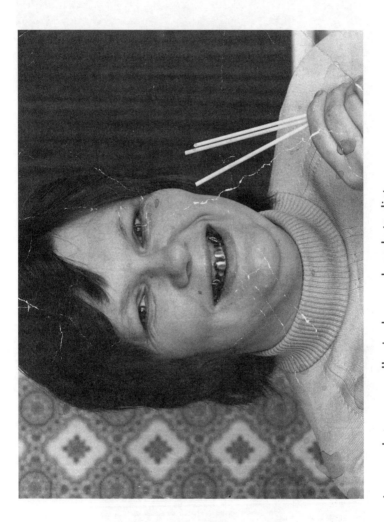

Jaws and straws - all wired up and ready to diet

Chapter 19

London bound

"Oh, look at that fat slob," I hear them say.
They look at me in such a way.
This huge, fat body, shuffling along,
Each painful step takes an age.
Inside my mind is utter rage at my
Inability to control my food intake.
When will my pain go away?

On one on my many occasions rummaging through paper-work, I came across a document relating to Stan's Civil Services pension, which was £25 per month. I realised that if Stan and I were not married, I would lose any right to this money, which didn't seem fair since I had been with Stan through some of the leanest years. I mentioned to the children about marrying their dad and they all thought it was a brilliant idea.

The wedding was a low-key affair, with one or two of Stan's relatives attending. And much to my horror, I found out later that Stan's pension would cease on his death and I would be entitled to just £2 per year!

One of the main pleasures I had in life was the television and I would spend endless hours watching children's programmes, omnibus editions of serials that I had already seen … anything, really. I did this while feeding my face in a constant gorge. A packet of biscuits would see me through a cartoon, a mountain of chips would accompany me through the latest happenings in Coronation Street.

One afternoon, I sat watching a documentary concerning the issue of dieting and the effects of stomach stapling. I was intrigued with the apparent success of this operation and wondered if this was what I had been looking for over the last 20 years. It seemed like an easy option and the idea was strengthened by an article I read in a magazine. It concerned a married couple and how their lives had changed for the better because of the operation.

I decided to write to Doctor Kark, who had been mentioned

in the documentary. He was based in London and was the pioneer of the operation, so I held little hope of receiving a reply.

It was about a month later when Stan handed me a letter. I looked at the postmark. London! But I didn't open it straight away because I was expecting the usual "Thank you for your letter but I am unable to consider you for this operation."

When I eventually plucked up the courage to open the letter, Stan looked at me as though I had finally flipped. My arms shot up in the air and the wobble of my fat ricocheted around my whole body.

"Stan, they want to see me, they want to see me about this operation!"

Stan's response was typical. "I'm not too sure about this one, duck."

This reaction brought me back down to earth but if the doctor was willing to see me, then I knew I was half way there.

After I had received the letter of confirmation for my visit to St Clementines Hospital, I had to face up to the fact that I would struggle to get there. My weight had created a very embarrassing problem for me. Not only was I immobile, but when I did move my sweat glands went into overdrive and I gave off a definite odour. My travelling difficulty had obviously crossed Stan's mind.

"How are you going to get there, Sylvia?"

"I'll have to go by coach," I replied, which was really the only possible way because I couldn't afford to go by train, as much as I would have liked to.

The next problem was what I was going to wear. I had no decent underwear and the only dress that was comfortable was like a huge green marquee.

So I knew that I would be going to this appointment bra-less, tights-less and in a shabby green tent. Thank heaven a friend had managed to buy me an enormous pair of underpants off the local market. It had become virtually impossible to find anything to fit me.

Stan arranged for his friend to take me to the bus station in his old Avenger. It was built like a tank and did not tilt to the side when my enormous bulk sat in it. Once again, Stan organised my packed food. Whatever I wanted I would get. I only had to say and it was there. He knew that I would eat as much as he provided and still have room for more.

I arrived at the bus station in plenty of time. When the coach pulled up I let the other passengers board first because I knew that they would all be gawping at my enormous frame. Then, the most embarrassing thing happened. I couldn't fit through the small doors of the coach and had to suffer the humiliation of being pushed through them sideways.

The next obstacle was finding a seat. Fortunately, the coach wasn't fully booked and I was able to have two seats to myself. I don't think that anyone would have wanted to sit with me anyway. I was so embarrassed about being pushed on to the bus that my perspiration had begun to filter through my dress. I was conscious of my body odour for the whole journey.

The trip was to take four and a half hours and the only thought that kept me going was that the doctor would have a sympathetic ear to my cause. I had to sit through the sly glances of the other passengers and I really did feel low and lonely. I felt like a freak and the other passengers probably considered me to be one.

The two seats that I took up were so uncomfortable, partly due to the fact that there was no possible space for me to move into a good position. My stomach touched my knees which were squashed up against the next seat. I must have looked as though I was about 18 months pregnant. At least if I had been, I wouldn't have received so many condescending looks.

Stan had done a good job of catering for my journey. I had plenty of sandwiches, crisps, sausage rolls and anything else that he could squeeze into the bag. It didn't take long before I began eating. Stan had packed enough food for getting there and back, but I knew that there wouldn't be a great deal left for the journey home.

I tried to disguise the fact that I was eating. I turned my face to the window so that the only people who could see me would be whizzing past at around 70 miles per hour. The irony of it is that I finished my 'snack' off with a can of diet drink. I kept my coat on all the way to London because I thought it would help to hide my frame. Who was I trying to kid?

The coach pulled into London and I waited for all the other passengers to disembark. The coach driver actually came to my rescue and helped me to step off the bus. I then had the task of finding my way to Sudbury Hill. By the time I got going in the right direction, I was in a right state. My legs were swollen and bright red from chafing together. Walking up that hill felt like trying to climb Mount Everest with a pair of crutches.

I arrived at St Clementines in a state of panic and asked the first person I saw to direct me to the nearest ladies' lavatories. I desperately wanted to wash my face and spray some much needed deodorant on my body. I looked a wreck. When I finished trying to convince myself that I looked half decent, I made my way to the reception area.

"I have an appointment with Dr Kark," I said and the receptionist advised me to sit down. She looked at me as though she could not comprehend the size of my body and said: "Doctor Kark will be with you shortly."

I was just starting to relax when I was ushered into the doctor's room by the receptionist and advised to get undressed. This was the height of embarrassment for me. I found it difficult myself to look at the never ending folds of fat, never mind letting a total stranger see them. I slowly started to peel off my clothes but as hard as I tried to drag this process out it still only took a few minutes. After all, I wasn't really wearing that much. I sat on the bed and the blubber was hanging everywhere. The veins in my legs were protruding so much they resembled a road atlas. I felt that the doctor's initial response was one of pity, and I can hardly blame him.

"Mrs Hurt, something should have been done for you years ago," he said.

"Well, I did have my mouth wired but after they were taken off I put all the weight back on and more besides. I think everyone, even the doctors, have lost faith in me."

He asked me if I suffered any recurring back problems and I told him that with a frame like mine my poor back was always in agony.

"I feel that you should be given priority for this operation, Mrs Hurt. Get dressed and we can discuss it further."

I shuffled off the table and began to dress myself. It was really difficult just to bend down to put my huge knickers on. When I finished, the doctor said: "Do you have an insurance plan, Mrs Hurt?"

"What do you mean, doctor?" I couldn't understand what this had to do with the operation.

He replied: "A health care plan."

AM I NOT A PERSON?

I smiled. "You must be joking. My financial state has gone past the stage of just coping. It's absolutely desperate!"

"I could get you into the hospital within two weeks if you are willing to pay."

"How much are we talking about, doctor?" I hoped that there would be some way that the price would be affordable to me. But his reply nearly knocked me off my seat.

"Two thousand pounds. That would include six days in this hospital and aftercare in Nottingham."

"I'm sorry, but that is so out of my reach." I was crying inside but I was trying to put on a brave face for this man. I so wanted him to say that he would do it for me.

"Since you don't have the finances to see this through, Mrs Hurt, I'm sorry to say that I am unable to treat you personally."

I felt totally deflated, but he continued: "However, there is currently a medical research programme going on at Northwick Park Hospital. I will pass your details over to my colleague there and he will send for you in due course. I believe you should be considered a priority."

I saw a ray of hope but I struggled to hold back the tears as I left St Clementines. Dr Kark was a very pleasant and genuine man. I understood his reasons for not being able to treat me and I was glad that he knew somebody who might help me.

I slowly trudged to the underground, my legs seeming to hurt more than ever. At the other end, I found a cafe and sat there with a cup of coffee and a mandatory bar of chocolate. As I ran things through my mind, I realised I was becoming very bitter.

Why should I be a pauper? Why was I such a slob? But these were rhetorical questions and I knew that I didn't have the answers. Who did? I detested myself for being such a failure. After all, if I had control of my body and my emotions, there would be no need for me to go through this pain and humiliation.

I left the cafe feeling desperate and depressed. Maybe I was wrong to, but I had pinned so many hopes on this visit to London. When I got to the bus station I was exhausted and my legs felt twice the size that they actually were. I needed some help to get me on to the bus again and I had to sit through the stares once more. I should have been used to it by now but it still hurt.

The first thing I did when I settled into my double seat was to kick off the tatty shoes that I was wearing. My feet had swollen and it felt as though they were screaming "hallelujah" when they were released. My toes were bleeding and the blisters on my heels had broken.

The bus was fairly busy on the way home and I felt guilty for taking up two seats but there was no way that any one would have been able to travel comfortably next to me. My only entertainment on the journey back was watching the other travellers shoot past on their coaches.

I only noticed slim bodies going past, accompanied by their slim partners. Everyone seemed just about perfect and I was making myself feel more and more downtrodden. I shut my eyes and tried to visualise myself with the perfect body ... well, society's perfect body. I tried to see myself on a beach wearing a nice little bikini. Fantasy land ...

"We will be pulling in for refreshments, 10 minutes please!" The bus driver's voice woke me from my dream. I didn't bother getting off. I didn't have any money anyway and it would save me a good deal of humiliation.

A lady passing by noticed that my feet were bleeding. "Here you are love, here's a damp tissue to wipe your feet." She smiled at me sympathetically and I smiled back. Little did she realise that I couldn't even reach my feet. When everyone had climbed back on to the coach, I began to doze. Then I felt a tap on my shoulder.

"Would you like a drink?" It was the kind lady who had given me the tissue.

"I'd love to have a drink, but I haven't got any money until I get back to Nottingham," I replied, feeling my colour rise.

"Don't you worry about that, it's only a coffee."

We made general conversation for a few minutes and then she returned to her seat. I was grateful to her for her genuine concern but I was getting a little fed up with sympathy. I needed people to talk to me for who I was and not because I was a walking wreck.

As we approached Nottingham, my mind came back to reality and wandered to its usual thoughts. Had Stan cooked me anything for tea? I was starving. I made my way to the nearest telephone box to ask Stan to come and fetch me because there was no way that I could face another bus journey that day. As soon as he answered, I told him to put my dinner on. He never asked me what I wanted but he always did something. The I waited in the Victoria Centre bus station, shoeless and being stared at. Hurry up, Stan.

Finally, he turned up. "How did it go?"

"I'm on the waiting list."

"Oh good," he replied. And that was that.

Over the next 12 months I made several trips to Northwick Park to see people who had had this operation. Their lives had certainly changed for the better but there were loads of side effects such as stomach cramps and vomiting. I waited and waited for a letter to tell me I was the next in line, but it never came. Due to a reduction in funding, the research programme had come to an end.

On reflection, I am quite pleased that I didn't have it done because I would not have been addressing the real problem - the cause of my pain.

Chapter 20

The flight of hope

To the outside world, happy families,
No-one ever knew what was happening to me.
Send to bed feeling hungry and sad.
Surely, I wasn't that bad?
Arms reaching out, Mum, but you are not there.
I feel absolute despair.

One night in November 1988, I was contemplating another massive binge when the telephone interrupted my thoughts. It was my sister, Annie. Between the international bleeps and her sobs, I was able to grasp that Mum was seriously ill and on a life support machine.

"She's going to die, Sylv, you know."

All I felt at that precise time was pity for Annie and an urgency to see Mum. I desperately wanted to ask her why she had been so awful to me and then I just might be able to offer forgiveness. Annie continued to sob and I told her I would definitely do my best to get to Oz. How, I didn't know. I was living on a budget way below the poverty line but I promised to return her call within a few hours. When Stan arrived home he was his usual self, rabbiting on about what he had been working on that day.

"Stan," I interrupted, "Mum's dying."

"I'm sure she won't pass away, Sylv, she's so strong."

"I have to go," I said.

"Where?" Stan asked, not really believing what he was hearing.

"Oz!"

"What with, Sylv? Face up to it, we have no money."

But I knew I had to get there. I made several calls to the help line on the local radio station, BBC Radio Nottingham, and enquired if any airlines did cheap flights to Oz. I would make a dozen stop-overs if I had to.

Within one hour of my phone call, my situation was on the local news and not long afterwards Oz Travel offered me a ticket on its maiden flight to Perth. I understood this was about 1000 miles from where I needed to be in Canberra but a few minutes later, the 'phone went again and it was Quantas Airlines, offering me a seat for £100 from Perth to Sydney. I couldn't believe it. The flight was several weeks away and I hoped Mum would survive. That same afternoon, I 'phoned Annie and she was beside herself with joy, but she still felt desperate.

"Sylv, I need you," she said.

"Well, I will be there soon."

John tried to console her. George and the rest of the family had made the trip up to the hospital. In our conversations, I told Annie that I didn't want to see two members of my family. She asked why and I told her.

She started to sob. "Yes Sylv, the same thing happened to me." I was gutted.

Annie assured me she would be at Sydney airport to pick me up and she would bring John along. It had been 20 years since I had seen either of them.

I had to keep reminding myself that I was on a mission, a mission of hope to ask Mum "Why?", to detach myself from the hurt, the anger, the loneliness. It was also to see John again, the part of me that was missing. As I write this, my heart skips a beat and I know the bond between John and me will never die.

I knew as soon as I had finished talking that I would eat. Oddly enough, as I pigged out on next week's rations, I knew that I had to try to reduce my size. I knew at the rate I was going I definitely would not fit into the airline seats.

I had about £100 to go with and I bought myself several dresses from the bargain shop Fords.

The morning of the departure came and I was no slimmer. I asked Stan to help me to squeeze into my all-in-one corset. The folds of skin were pushed together and my legs were touching each other. I felt a little discomfort but it didn't matter. I was on my way.

Stan had decided to come to Luton to wave me off. Mark took both of us with my luggage to the Victoria Centre bus depot. Lisa understood my urgency to get to Oz and wished me well for my journey.

But she still said to me: "I know it's hard to accept, Mum, but everyone has to die sometime. I know it must be really hard for you not knowing what is happening and not being able to see her, but life must go on."

I began to think about Lisa's words and wondered whether Mum would pass on before I arrived in Oz. Stan and I boarded the coach to Luton. I could not believe that I was about to embark on a trip to Oz. Stan had catered for my needs again on the food front and had even packed a flask of tea. As I sipped it in between my sarnies, I could see Stan looking at me longingly. He kept stroking my hand.

"I'm going to miss you, ducky, while you're gone."

"Look after the boys well," I said, but I knew the boys would be looking after Stan.

We arrived at Luton two and a half hours before my departure time and I really thought my body was going to cave in through not being able to breathe. My shoulders were on fire because the straps on my corset were digging in. I began to feel angry with myself for trying to conform to what people wanted me to look like.

Stan carried my case and as we approached the check-in desk I was brimming with excitement. It must have looked as if I was on a camping trip with all my hand luggage which was, of course, full of food. I didn't want to hang around and I said my farewells to Stan. He had a strange look on his face and I knew what was bothering him. I would be out of his control for four whole weeks. He reached over to kiss me and I froze and pulled away.

I walked through to the waiting area and my flight number was soon announced. I waited a while then followed on. As I boarded the small steps to the plane, I thought the people behind me must have thought that an elephant in a frock was in front of them.

The captain introduced himself to everyone while I was directed to my seat. I tried desperately to squeeze into it as quickly as I could but the passenger next to me was not impressed. She only had an inch to spare. I felt embarrassed but there was not a lot I could do. The lady that had the misfortune of sitting next to me soon moved further up the plane which damaged my self-esteem somewhat. The main thing was that I was on my way and there had been no hitches.

I sat at the tail end of the plane. I had never flown in my life before and I was going to be on this flight for 28 hours. The plane moved down the runway and I began to feel like my stomach had left my body. We were soon airborne and I began to turn things over in my mind. I was sure that once I saw Mum I would soon forget about my inhibitions.

It wasn't long before I began to wonder when food would be served. Clearly, my humiliation never lasted very long. Perhaps if it did I would have been in control long ago. I was slightly embarrassed at having to ask for a belt extension, but there was more to come.

After five or 10 minutes of being airborne, the drinks trolley came down the aisle. I had never really tasted a short but I just treated myself to an orange. After all, I didn't want to arrive in Oz slurring my words, although a little Dutch courage would not have gone amiss. There would be a lot of the past to hit me in the face when I arrived and that was one side of this visit that I was not looking forward to.

Not long after the drinks, I heard the clatter of pots and knew it wouldn't be long before I could feed myself. I gave a big sigh because I didn't know how much longer I could have held on without delving into my bag for a choccie bar. I had already tried the fold-away table in anticipation just to check it would fold over my huge knees. It came as no great surprise when it wouldn't.

When the meal was eventually served, I had to sit to one side and use the table on the empty seat for my food. It was a real shock when I got the meal. Here I was, with my stomach thinking my throat had been cut, and they had served me a meal not much larger than I would prepare for a child.

Of course, this was my opinion seen through gluttony-tinted glasses. To anyone else, the meal would have been more than adequate. My food didn't even touch the sides. I had finished it before the majority of the passengers had been served their meals and I was frantically rummaging through my bag for some chocolate which was rapidly running out.

I just happened to look across the plane to see a well-dressed lady staring at me. Then she whispered to her husband and I knew it was about the way I was eating. I had used the fork like a shovel with my main meal and now I was cramming my mouth full of chocolate. It worked like a dream, a really effective anaesthetic, better than any of the useless drugs I was given in all my hospital stays.

AM I NOT A PERSON?

I was offered coffee but declined because I knew I would be unable to use the loo. Stan had already drilled it into me that there was not a great deal of room in them and I was afraid that once I got in there I would not be able to get out again.

I tried to block out the nagging pain that developed in my side telling me that I needed to go and I attempted to doze for a while. By the time we had reached our first stop-over, I thought my stomach was going to explode. My insides were on fire.

We stopped in Singapore and I told the stewardess I didn't want to get off the plane. She looked quite surprised but I just wanted everyone else to get off so that I could go to the toilet. When I finally got there, I had never felt so relieved in all my days.

By the time we reached Bahrain, my feet had swollen up like balloons and I desperately needed to stretch my legs, if they were still functioning. When I got off the plane, a couple asked if I would like to have a look around with them and I jumped at the chance. I really didn't fancy the idea of walking around on my own. The gun-toting soldiers looked so menacing. The heat was unbelievable and it wasn't long before I was perspiring profusely. I felt more uncomfortable than ever and was pleased when I boarded the plane for the last leg of my journey.

Now I began to get huge butterflies in my stomach. I couldn't help wondering what Mum's reaction would be when she saw me. Would the rejection still be there? I tried again to nod off but every time I did I saw the eyes of my abusers haunting me, their leering grins, their sexual organs ready to hurt me. I awoke with a jolt as an announcement told us to fasten our seat belts.

This was it. I had made it but boy, did I need a decent meal. My mind focused on the barbecues that Annie had promised me. I arrived at Perth, had a coffee and booked into a motel for the night. But I couldn't sleep so I put the TV on to pass the time. I phoned Annie and told her I wouldn't be waiting two days for my connection. My times had been altered and I would be in Sydney the following day.

When I arrived at the airport I felt like I could not have managed much longer without a meal. It was like I was on the verge of starvation. My compulsion had followed me to Oz and it was reaching its peak. I was convinced that if I didn't eat soon I would collapse. I'd managed to get to Sydney a few hours earlier than Annie was expecting me, so I 'phoned her.

When she arrived I was overjoyed. I simply cannot put into words how I felt. My body was cheering and my eyes would not stop dropping tears of happiness. On the other hand, I had to keep reminding myself why I was there. Annie was sobbing and as I glanced over her shoulder I saw John in the distance, walking slowly towards us. I let go of Annie and flung my arms around him. I cried uncontrollably but John was motionless. He had no tears at all but I knew in my heart what he was feeling. It had always been that way.

Then John said: "Bloody hell, Sylvia, you've put some weight on since I last saw you."

"Pain, John," was all I could say.

He seemed to ignore my comment and we all made our way to the car. I asked how Mum was getting on and they said she was at home. She had been released from hospital that day. While the whole point of my trip was to see Mum, it was absolute heaven seeing Annie and John again.

"Gee, I've missed you, Sylv," Annie said. "It's so good to see you.

The conversation never stopped that evening. We talked about anything and everything while John did his best to get a word in. The thing that amazed me was the difference in lifestyle that they all enjoyed in Oz. I realised there and then that life is what you make it and I was going to do my best to achieve more in my life when I got back to England.

I had no idea what that would involve but I knew my main priority was to address the real problem of my compulsive eating. I knew it would be hard and at times so very painful but I was the only who could do it. The attitude of the Aussies to obese people was so refreshing and surprised me. Although it seemed to be a place that promoted health, locals did not treat obese people any differently. This was the first place where I'd felt totally at ease. I even went swimming and didn't feel like a beached whale. The only thing I didn't like in Oz was the price of chocolate.

I stayed at Annie's for two days then was driven eight hours to Mum's in Canberra. I felt a bit more awake after getting over my jet lag but I had mixed emotions. I just couldn't contemplate the idea of rejection again.

We arrived at Mum's place in a nice little suburb. Her flat was compact. I made my way up the drive and the door opened. For a moment, I froze and stared apprehensively at this frail old lady with her deep brown eyes staring back, her tears flowing.

"Hi, Sylv. Good trip?" she asked and showed me into her lounge. It was a shock for me to see her like this. She had always been so dominant and now she looked frail and needy. I was trying to hold my emotions back but Mum was doing enough crying for both of us. I told her not to upset herself and to stay calm. She had only been out of hospital for two days [I had been told she was given the last rites twice] and here she was smiling at me through tear-stained cheeks. I knew my younger brother George lived not far way and it wasn't long before he turned up.

This was part of my childhood I had not seen for more than two decades and it was extremely weird. I had been very close to George and it hurt me so much when he emigrated. He is now an Aussie citizen. He hadn't altered much, just aged a little, but hadn't we all?

George had had a hard time in Oz. His first marriage ended on the rocks without him ever realising things were going sour. I felt for him. He invited me over to stay with him for a few days and I told him that I would after Mum and I had been together for a couple of weeks.

I had a wonderful time there. George came over most days and took me on many sightseeing trips. His wife Katrina made me feel so welcome. On many occasions, we would all be laughing and joking, with Mum joining in, but rarely did we talk about the past and never about my pain. All I felt for Mum at this point was compassion and pity. I couldn't hurt her the way she had hurt me and I couldn't face the rejection if I approached her about the past.

After a week, Mum seemed to have a new lease of life. One afternoon after sitting out in her back garden, she went to sort her bedroom out. Then I saw her making her way to the dustbin with what looked like a very old family portrait of the kids and her and Dad.

"Mum," I said, "what are you doing with that?" I walked over and took it from her. "You can't do that."

AM I NOT A PERSON?

It was as if she was cutting her ties of motherhood completely. I instantly put the photo in my suitcase. As painful as the picture was to me, I had to have it.

While I was there, I never raised the past with Mum but I was hurting so much that I started to mutilate myself again. I felt ill at ease because Mum had been talking to one of my abusers. Now she was hurting me in another way.

I decided to end my stay and travel back to Annie's. I gave Mum a hug when I left but the coldness was still there. I had said my farewells to George the day before I left Mum's. It tore me apart to leave him.

When I arrived at Annie's after a long coach journey, a meal was once again on my mind. I was angry with myself for travelling halfway around the world and saying nothing to Mum about what was ruining my life but Annie was there to give me support with food and more food. For a while, my pain had gone.

John turned up one day while I was there and announced: "I'm taking you all out for the day to Manley." It was the best day of my visit, mainly because there was lots of food involved.

John took us to a Chinese restaurant which was a whole new experience to me and I was in my element. It was self-service and, needless to say, I had more than my money's worth. John was footing the bill and all the drinks were on him. My only wish was that my children could have been there to share this moment and my family with me. I didn't dare contemplate meeting Neville and Danny while I was in Oz.

During my stay at Annie's, I received a 'phone call from Danny's wife which was full of insults and abuse. The stupid thing was that I had never met the woman. Neville had 'phoned Annie several times and said that he was trying to build bridges. The past was rearing its ugly head again and I couldn't handle it. So I ate and ate.

I knew Annie was finding it hard to accept that Mum dragged her away to live in Oz when she was just 14. Annie also has a weight problem and a compulsion with food but she has a good business head on her shoulders. Her weight is not a major issue in her life and she is accepted the way she is.

My four weeks just flew by and my days left in Oz were now down to hours. I had decided not to cry buckets when I left. I knew saying goodbye would play havoc with us emotionally so

AM I NOT A PERSON?

I put my feelings into verse and it flowed out. Annie and her husband had loaded my case up and Annie had given me an art nouveau clock. I hoped Customs wouldn't think that I had a bomb in my case.

My hand luggage was loaded with stuff I had picked up off the flea market and one of the glass bowls now takes pride of place on my ornamental shelf at home. Funnily enough, it's exactly the same as one of the neighbours'.

Our trip to the airport was a quiet affair because the conversation was non-existent. We arrived at Sydney with time to spare and Annie bought me a coffee. I started to cry when Annie and I approached the departure gates. Annie had her tissues out and I tried to work out why life had been so cruel to me. Mostly, the four weeks in Oz had been bliss and I just didn't want it to end. Annie had been fantastic to me. Nothing had been too much trouble for her.

I stood near the gates and Annie sobbed uncontrollably: "Please don't go. Please, Sylv."

She reached out and hugged me tight. My heart was aching. It was as if I was once again leaving a limb behind [John had said his farewells the day before and, once again, he couldn't cry]. I hugged Annie to say a final farewell but no words would come out. I handed her the verses that I had written and asked her to pass George's on to him. He had work commitments and couldn't see me off. Or was it too painful?

As I walked towards the departure gate, I glanced around and Annie was sobbing in her husband's arms. I mouthed: "Bye Annie, I love you," then went through the gate in a stream of tears.

Soon, I had to think about my nine-hour wait in Cairns. I had no money so I was unable to go anywhere. I found out later that the Great Barrier Reef was a 30-minute coach ride away but I couldn't go. A chance of a lifetime missed. While I sat in Cairns airport, I began to reflect on how my life could change for the better. Then, suddenly, it was boarding time. I was relieved. I would be able to have a drink at long last.

My thoughts turned to home as I sat waiting for take-off and what might have been if I had emigrated when I had the chance. The month I'd been with my family seemed like heaven. It is a memory I will cherish for the rest of my life. Annie had said that we should never be parted for so many years again but I think we may both be pensioners next time we meet.

After take-off, I was once again beginning to feel angry with myself. I had not achieved the point of my trip to Oz and I was still hurting. When the drinks trolley came around I had a whisky, something I had never done before. The meals were soon being served and I had no back-up rations this time, so I was hungry.

There were loads of empty seats on this flight, so I lay down across three of them and nodded off. The time seemed to just fly by. We had one stop-over at Singapore and again I decided to stay on board. Very soon, or so it seemed, I was back on home soil. I hoped Stan had not forgotten to check my arrival times.

I disembarked from the plane, laden with hand luggage, and waited for my suitcase. When I came through Customs [the clock did not cause an international crisis!] I looked for Stan and there he was, with his toothless grin. As I approached him, he reached out to kiss me.

"I've missed you, duck. How are you?"

"Fine, Stan. I didn't want to come back." I seemed distant from Stan and really couldn't say very much. I felt empty again because that other part of me, John, was missing.

While we waited for the bus to arrive, Stan delved into a carrier bag and pulled out several cheese and onion sandwiches with pickle on. I stuffed the sarnies in my grateful mouth and Stan told me to take my time.

"I'm starving, Stan. How's the boys?"

"No problem, Sylv.

I dozed off on the coach for a couple of hours, no doubt from jet lag, and we soon arrived at the bus station where Mark was waiting. When I got home, there to greet me was a newly decorated kitchen. The house was spotless and Stan was looking for all the praise he could get.

I couldn't take it away from him, he had done a brilliant job. I sat in my usual throne-like chair, thinking once again that I had achieved the impossible. I had made it to Oz against all the odds.

Chapter 21

'Stuck' in a 25st nightmare

My son tells me off for the way I eat,
Frustration setting in.
Food anaesthetises the pain for a while
And then I'm spoken to like a child by loved ones
Who are supposed to care.
I will win my battle and I will fight.
This compulsion will not ruin my life.

Around this time, I put in for another move. By now, Mark and Carl were 13 and 14 and doing very well at school. Lisa had become a student at High Pavement doing her A levels when we had a letter to say that we could move into a house at Wollaton. Posh Wollaton!

It was an old house and very basic but I could see it had potential. We weren't far from the school but my immediate neighbours, who were retired, took an instant dislike to us. They wouldn't speak and everything we did they reported to the Council. We erected a new shed and we were reported. My sons didn't play any loud music or make a noise outside but still the neighbours hated this intrusion by the younger generation. There was only one lady three doors away who thought that I was worth talking to.

My weight was taking its toll but I had still decided to apply for a job at the Queens Medical Centre. Again, Stan was nervous about the fact that I was not going to be controlled by him. I had my interview and was informed that due to being overweight I needed a medical which I passed. I also got myself a little cleaning job in a bungalow where I was my own boss.

I was thrilled to be earning again. As well as the cleaning job, I worked overtime at Queens because I wanted to buy my home. I told Lisa and the boys and they were pleased for me.

I applied for a valuation and the right to buy and am delighted to say that I got it for peanuts. Now, I could hold my head up.

I felt thrilled to think I had been labelled sub-normal and now

AM I NOT A PERSON?

here I was owning my own home. I was so proud of myself. For the next 12 months I never looked back. and even though my eating was still out of control, I was able to hold two jobs down. But there was soon another hurdle to got over.

I was feeling more and more tired and my headaches had become really bad. I made an appointment with my doctor who found something blister-like at the base of my spine.

"I'm sorry to inform you, Mrs Hurt, that you have shingles."

I was off work for months. I also had other medical problems and was advised to pack in work on a long-term basis. But the more time I spent at home, the more flashbacks I got. I was in inner turmoil and it was a silent torture.

Mark and Carl were good lads but even they started to question my food intake. I would tell them it was my body and I could do what I wanted with it! Although he sometimes passed comment, Stan would cater for my every need on the food front. He would give me lots of fried eggs with tomatoes swimming in fat. Not surprisingly, I was becoming more and more immobile and Stan had to do most things for me, including the shopping. At times, I would demolish the week's supply of crisps and chocolate in one day.

Lisa had left college to start her first job and was now going steady with her boyfriend. I was so proud of her. Some time later she told me she was going to have my first grandchild and I was delighted. I offered my services if she wanted to keep her career going and she kept me to my word when Heather was born. I started looking after her at nine weeks old.

Lisa and Andy were living with me until they had saved enough money for a deposit on a house and when Heather was one, they bought their own home. Heather was dropped off to me every day. She was crawling but my own movements were just as slow. I knew Lisa was very concerned about my weight and my health but she never hurt me about it. When Heather was a toddler, Lisa had asked me to take her down town so she could show Heather off to her office friends.

I got ready to meet her and Stan helped me to put my split moccasins on. I took a slow walk to the bus stop, squeezed on to the bus and within 30 minutes we were off again and waiting for Lisa. When she appeared, she picked Heather up and told me how nicely I had dressed her.

"I will sit here, ducky, until you come out," I said.

AM I NOT A PERSON?

Shortly, she came back up the road with Heather and told me she had finished for the day. She was on flexi time. But as we stood there I could see a look of anguish on her face.

"What's the matter, Lisa?"

"Look, Mum, I can't give you a lift home in my Mini. The suspension won't take your weight."

I knew Lisa was right but once again I felt a sense of rejection and sadness. Lisa and Heather went on their way and I slowly walked to the bus stop. On my way, I went into the newsagents, bought crisps and chocolate and ate them as I sat sobbing on the bus back. For a short while, I could block out the truth and the reality.

When I arrived home, Stan asked: "Where's Heather?"

I told him what had happened and he told me Lisa was right. Then not long after, he would bring my 'dustbin lid' in with my cholesterol nightmare on it. Then he'd say I was a fat slob and constantly pinch my body, which by now weighed 25st.

"If you could lose weight, Sylv, you would be lovely."

One day, Stan had to fetch the doctor to me because I had picked up some bug that was going around. When the doctor arrived he told me point blank that if I didn't lose weight I would die within six months. I started to cry. I wanted to live, I really did. I wanted to see Lisa and the boys married and I wanted to see my grandchildren grow up. But still I ate.

Heather was a good child and highly intelligent. I would sing her favourite nursery rhymes to her and teach her colours and simple sums. Even at such a tender age she would bring her toys to me because she understood I couldn't get about.

Every night when I retired to bed I would sob myself to sleep. I was angry with myself for not being in control and I worked out that if I could be in control for just one day, it was worth a try. I decided to write on paper at every opportunity 'YOU DESERVE TO MATTER', hoping it would make a difference.

I enrolled Heather into a playgroup when she was three, even though it took me an age to get there. It was her right to go to playgroup and she loved it.

On our return home one dismal day, Heather asked: "Can I have a bath, Nanna?"

"Of course, love." It was our special time together.

As I undressed she looked me up and down.

"Why are you fat, Nanna?"

AM I NOT A PERSON?

"Because I'm a pig, darling."

She stood for a while thinking about this, then got into the bath with me.

After her little play with the sponge and toys, I asked her if she would like to do some paintings so she got out and dried herself. But then disaster struck. I had pulled the plug out and as I tried to manoeuvre out of the bath, I realised I was stuck.

I could move neither up nor down. Heather got dressed and I asked her to look for Grandad. But Stan had gone to the shops. Eventually, he came walking up the drive and she ran to him.

"Grandad, Grandad!" She grabbed his hand and guided him upstairs.

I was shivering. I was so cold. Stan put a bedspread over me then started shouting at me: "You will have to lose weight, Sylvia! You can't go on like this!"

I was humiliated.

"Lisa will have to help you," Stan said. "You will have to wait for Lisa."

"How long?" I whispered, totally embarrassed.

Heather had brought a reading book up and through my shivers, I started to read to her. Then I heard Stan telling someone about my plight and soon Lisa was coming upstairs.

She peered around the door and told me in a stern voice: "God, Mum, you will have to lose weight. It's not fair on Heather."

I whispered: "All right duck, I will, I will. Just get me out."

Stan got behind me and Lisa pulled. I heard my skin release from the sides with the sound of a plunger. I was free from my embarrassing nightmare and I shuffled to my bedroom, wanting to crawl away and hide my shame. The shame of eating, the shame of letting Lisa down. When I came downstairs later, Lisa offered to pay for me to join a slimming club of my choice.

"But they thrive on your misery," I said.

"It's the only way forward, Mum. Do you want Heather to be without a Nan?"

"No, no I don't," I said and started to cry again.

"It's no use crying, Mum, that won't solve it will it?"

I knew Lisa was right but she didn't know why I was this size. I wanted desperately to unburden myself of my inner torment and tell somebody but the fear was still alive within me.

"Well, Mum, when are you going to the slimming club?"

AM I NOT A PERSON?

I switched off. I felt it was too drastic. But Stan was hovering. "You will have to do it," he said.

"Why? So you can ogle my body?" I snapped, but I could see Lisa was upset. It was her Dad I was speaking to and she didn't understand my anger.

"Do you know Sylv," Stan said, "you are going to die."

"I know, Stan. I know."

Pension day was a Thursday and on one occasion Stan informed me that we were going to Bulwell and he had offered to give a neighbour a lift.

Stan had a two-door hatchback. I pushed myself into the back and our friend sat in the front. We arrived at Bulwell market within 10 minutes and my friend got out. But I was well and truly stuck, sandwiched between the front and back seats. Stan's anger had boiled over. He started to shout abuse at me while he was searching furiously for his spanners to unscrew the back seat.

He yelled: "You fat cow! We might have to get lifting gear to get you out!"

"I know, Stan," I whispered. "Just pack it in."

Stan's shouting had drawn a crowd and I began to think I was in some sort of circus. He was trying to release the nuts on the seat when there was an almighty thud. The seat fell back and I was stretched out. Everyone was staring at me, I was so embarrassed. I lay there, looking at the sky, with Stan pulling me to one side and yelling: "Bend your legs, Sylv. Come on, help me!"

He was so cross with me. He got hold of my legs which were like lumps of concrete and pushed them around. I was free. As I sat there humiliated and degraded, the crowd started to disappear. I gritted my teeth and said: "Don't you ever shout at me like that again, Stan."

"Well, do something about your weight, then."

I got out of the car and shuffled my frame to the shop to buy some chocolate and crisps. I stood cramming the sweets and savouries in my mouth when Stan appeared as if from nowhere.

"Sylvia! I'll tell Lisa, I mean it."

"Well tell her," I yelled. I was angry. I felt like a child again. Nobody knew my inner torment and this man who was supposed to love me was bringing it all to the surface. By the

150

AM I NOT A PERSON?

time we got home, Stan had carried on so much about my weight that I felt ill. I thought I might even be having a heart attack or something, it was that bad.

Stan hastily fetched the doctor whose first words were: "Mrs Hurt, you really will have to lose weight. You will die in months if you don't do something."

I knew I was on borrowed time but I knew what death was like. I felt like I had been crucified so many times.

My life was simply going nowhere. I was eating and eating and the more I ate the more worthless I felt through my inability to control it. After one of my mega binges, as I sat slumped in the chair, it suddenly dawned on me that it was my birthday in the morning ... 7 April 1990. I had outlived the six months my doctor had given me. Maybe that was good news, but I knew it meant every day could be my last.

I knew that I didn't want to die. I went to bed feeling angry with myself, angry that I had let myself down so badly. The next thing I knew it was 6.30am on 7 April. Someone was singing "Happy birthday to you." I knew that sweet voice was Heather's. She came in and gave me a big kiss and a hug then handed me my card.

Lisa came in next, but her arms were empty. She usually bought me nice things from Marks & Spencer or Jessop & Son, the Nottingham branch of John Lewis. She sat down on the bed and her eyes met mine. I could see so much pain in them. She hesitated then said: "Mum, I'm not buying you a prezzie. Well, I am, but it's a different type."

I looked at her, wondering what was coming next.

"I will pay for you to join a slimming club as a birthday present. You know we all love you, Mum, and we want you to be around us for some time to come."

My tears just flowed. Despite my fears of losing weight, I told Lisa I would try to find a club to join and she said she wanted to see my record book on a regular basis. I began to feel like a child again, but the difference was I knew Lisa loved me dearly. I loved all my family. If only I could tell them about my pain.

Some days later, Lisa arrived home at her usual time of 5.30 and I had a cup of coffee waiting when she walked through the door. I was keen to let her know that I had been in touch with a slimming club.

AM I NOT A PERSON?

"Well, Mum, have you made contact with anyone?"

"Yes, duck. Yes. At Rise Park. I'm going there tomorrow."

I told Lisa what the fee was and she left the money for me. The next day, I tried desperately to find a dress to fit me but the only one was a 30 plus that just went over my body. I knew the continuing destruction of my body was definitely going to kill me. This compulsion had to stop or I would die.

Then came the day to attend the class. Mark and Carl had vehicles so I knew I would be able to get a lift from Wollaton to Top Valley, which was about 10 minutes drive. Wouldn't I?

Carl arrived home. He had his date on his mind as he dressed and started to put gel on his hair.

"Can you give me a lift, Carl?"

"No," was his stern reply. "I've just put bucket seats in and they won't take your weight. I don't want them damaging." I felt rejected but I knew that he was right.

Mark had just finished his tea. I plucked up the courage and asked him: "Will you run me to Rachel's [a friend who lived near the club]?"

"Yes, Mum, but you will have to lay in the back. The front seats won't hold you."

This was humiliation of the worst kind but it didn't stop me eating. To be honest, the only thing on my mind was food. After I had filled my food bags for a binge on the way up to the class, I walked out to Mark's van. He opened the doors but when I sat on the floor, the back end of the van did a nose-dive.

"God, Mum!" Mark yelled. "You are so bloody fat! You've just got to lose weight!"

Once again, I felt such a failure. Even the children I adore were fed up of the sight of my enormous body. Mark told me to lie down, then he lifted my legs up and told me to shuffle my body. The bare floor scratched my back. I just lay there like a corpse when he set off, then I heard Mark say: "God, Mum, the van won't pick up speed with you in it!"

I shuffled out of Mark's van and to Rachel's door. She always treated me with the ultimate respect and never made me feel inadequate. I had confided in her over the years about my compulsion and as we sat having coffee I told her I was about to join a slimming club 10 minutes walk from her house. But it took me the best part of an hour to get there.

AM I NOT A PERSON?

While I was walking up the hill, I was stuffing my face with scones, crisps etc. My gluttony was beyond belief. By now, my legs were chafing and starting to bleed. I had decided to rest on a bollard and when I glanced up I could see the community centre. My heart was pounding, and for various reasons.

I thought for one instant that it was going to give up on me and I knew I really had to do something. This was my last chance. I eventually made it to the slimming club and when I opened the door the session was in full swing. All heads turned to greet me.

"Can I help you?" a voice chimed.

"Er ... I've just come to join your class."

"Yes, love. Come and sit down."

I slowly walked over to a seat. I was in so much pain. My legs were throbbing and as I put my weight on the chair I could feel it giving way. I immediately got up and sat on the stage. My legs were dangling down like tree trunks and I thought to myself that while I didn't want the body beautiful, I did want to be able to walk. At the end of the class I was pulled to one side and the counsellor explained the diet plan. Inside, I was hurting. I didn't need slimming clubs. I knew that if only I could unburden myself I would be able to control my eating. I got on the scales and was told I weighed exactly 25st.

"Don't worry, luvvy, we will help you get rid of this weight."

I was given my record book and told to drink plenty of water. When I left the club, I knew exactly what to do. I needed to rid myself of all my pain.

I wasn't making excuses but I knew that if my self-esteem was higher and I felt as if I mattered, the food would become secondary. I would be in full control.

I arrived back at Rachel's and she asked how I went on. She knew that I hated slimming clubs. I suppose if the support is there they can work for some people, but I felt that the scales were constantly being manipulated to show good weight loss one week, not so good the next. Nevertheless, Lisa had paid and given me a chance and I was going to try to lose weight. Mark arrived to pick me up and, again, I lay in the back of his van.

When I got home I went straight to bed. Tomorrow was another day and I knew now that I deserved to matter. I was definitely going to make an effort to be in control of my life.

AM I NOT A PERSON?

I was looking forward to seeing Lisa the next morning to show her I was making an effort. She arrived early and peered through the door with her radiant smile.

"Hi, Mum."

I held my slimming club book up and she ran over to me and gave me a hug and kiss.

"You can do it, you know, Mum."

I knew it would be the biggest battle of my life emotionally and God knows I no longer wanted to die. I decided healthy eating was the key but I just couldn't cope with the club.

Nevertheless, I started to keep a diary of my very own battle of the bulge.

11 May 1990

Really pleased that I managed to get through yesterday. I didn't eat anything that was bad. I keep telling myself that the only person I will be hurting if I give in is myself. It seems to be working. So I have given myself a pat on the back for being good. I'm going to prove that the last few weigh-ins haven't been one-off occasions.

23 May 1990

Weighed in at 22st 3lbs. I had done it. I was on the way. Carol was pleased and told me I was on the road to success.

30 May 1990

This week has been a shocker. I haven't stopped eating. I've eaten everything in sight. I am a failure once again.

I was put on the scales and it was no great surprise to find that I had not lost any weight. It wasn't too bad, though, because I hadn't put any on either.

The weeks are slipping by and I am not being stern enough when it comes to following my eating plan. I just cannot seem to get my mind back on the right track. I have got to make a bigger effort.

6 June 1990

My bulk is causing me a major headache. I have gained weight once more but I am not going to give in to my negative thoughts.

My mind keeps telling me that I can't do it and so what if I am fat? But I don't want to be fat. My weight has gone back up to 23st 6lbs. Will I fail on my eating plan again? Tomorrow, I must put my day's food out and not eat anymore.

AM I NOT A PERSON?

13 June 1990
23st 5lbs. I know it is only a pound loss, but I feel happier. Carol so rightly pointed out that a pound is better than nothing and it is a step in the right direction.

20 June 1990
22st 1lb. I seem to be going well at the moment and I am thinking positive. I gave myself a little treat today. I went to Clarendon College and had my hair permed by one of the students. I feel like a million dollars. I also enrolled at the college to learn how to use a word processor because I need a new interest. The busier I am, the better.

27 June 1990
Weight stayed the same. Not too disheartened. Carol tells me I am bound to have some weeks when I won't lose anything.

4 July 1990
21st 12lbs. I cannot put into words how I feel, but elated would start to describe my emotions. I appear to be losing the wedges. I think I am going to give you a miss for a while, diary.

Chapter 22

The walk of life

Life's for living, that's what they say.
I'm doing a walk for life today.
Twenty-five miles, a major task.
I really don't know how long I will last.

Stan was still eating junk and I had to be so firm with myself. It was a constant battle saying no to him about food but I had to do it. I started to feel more positive and decided to keep my mind busy. I so desperately wanted my children to remember me and if I did die, I wanted them to have something of me. I started to write about my life and this book is the result. I also expressed my feelings through poetry, painting and sculpting.

I was constantly longing for junk food with lots of fat, but I knew that once I had some I would be out of control again and the guilt would take over.

I had reduced my weight considerably but I just didn't dare look at myself in the mirror. I had the odd slip, such as a bag of chips, but I am human. By 10 November 1990 my weight was still causing me a major problem. I was gradually putting weight back on, losing 4lbs, putting 6lbs on.

A year later, I started to lose weight again but I couldn't cope with my slim figure. I needed help with my inner pain, not a diet. At one stage, I had lost 8st but felt ill at ease, especially when men gave me compliments. I looked a different person and the club entered me for the regional finalist of the year. Although I didn't want to win, I now own a trophy that says 'South Notts Slimmer of the Year 1991'.

I felt fit and able for the first time in years and heard of an annual walk in Nottingham called the Trent Walk. I wanted to do it and filled my form out. Then I was asked to go into the local Radio Trent studios to be interviewed about my walk and my amazing weight loss.

The biggest challenge in my life was trying to survive my obesity. And for a while, I felt I had it under control. I started to believe that I could achieve far more in life and I craved to do something worthwhile and to help others in some way. To me, the Trent Walk was the ultimate challenge.

To walk 25 miles would be a major achievement and I knew this was what I wanted and what I needed to do. Not only would it make me feel good about myself, but I would be helping to raise funds for charities.

I wasn't sure if I would manage the full 25 miles but I was going to have a good try. Just to walk four miles would be amazing, considering how incredibly immobile I had been. But first, I had the problem of getting a Trent Walk tee-shirt that would fit me!

I told all my friends about my ultimate challenge and got plenty of sponsors. I was proud of myself and I hadn't even made it to the starting line! Lisa told me she would come to see me off. I wanted to arrive at the Market Square early to get a feel of the event. The Lord Mayor was there and loads of balloons were let into the air. The atmosphere was electric. We had been blessed with a beautiful, clear evening.

Everyone was smiling and you could almost smell the enthusiasm. While the walkers began to congregate and after I had collected my number tag, Lisa took a photo. She also gave me a few things that I might need, such as extra socks and plasters. I felt confident that I could do the walk and I hoped my feet and body would rise to the challenge.

Lisa and I sat on the Council House steps and discussed tactics. She advised me not to go too fast and to treat it as a steady stroll. She reminded me again that it wasn't a race and told me that if I felt I had had enough, I should pack it in. I reassured her that I would do just that.

I had a packet of fruit pastilles to keep me going. I couldn't wait to get started and to soften up my new trainers, then a voice came over the tannoy: "All walkers to make their way to the start line."

It was to be a staggered start so that we wouldn't be falling over each other. I was in the third bunch and when my turn came, I moved to the front eagerly. I waved cheerio to Lisa and she shouted back: "Good luck, Mum, you show 'em how it's done."

I smiled back and my adrenaline was flowing. We were soon on the way and I set off at a brisk pace. I didn't want to kill myself but at the same time I didn't want to trail too far behind.

AM I NOT A PERSON?

I managed to catch up with two ladies who had done the Trent Walk in the past.

"This is my first attempt at this walk," I said. "I thought I would give it a go." I told them that I had lost a considerable amount of weight but I didn't go into too much detail. I didn't want to bore them. One of the ladies didn't mind talking, though, and she really opened her heart to me.

"I'm doing this walk for my daughter," she said. "She was taken from me when she was 16 years old with leukaemia. I know she would want me to do something. The money I raise is going towards research."

I could feel my eyes welling with tears and responded with a tremble in my voice: "Do you think you will finish the walk then?"

It was a silly question, really. I could see bravery and determination written all over this woman's face. If anyone could help me to complete this walk, it was her.

We had walked about a mile and a half and were approaching Trent Bridge. I was still going at a remarkable pace and the novelty had not yet worn off. However, I was longing to see a refreshment point. I kept getting this image of myself crawling along the road, croaking: "Water ... water," and just as I reached the refreshment point it would disappear like a mirage in one of those classic black and white comedies. This thought kept me smiling.

"Did you bring an orange?" somebody shouted. They could obviously tell that I was starting to flag. My fringe was getting damp and sticking to my forehead. I just carried on walking.

"Got to keep going, you can do it, Sylv," I kept repeating under my breath. I was convinced that I would not make it to the end of Trent Bridge but I kept trying to put my best foot forward.

As we approached the next leg, the lady that I had been walking with started to move in front. She had been trying to gee me up for the last half hour but my pace was still fading. She obviously needed to get a move on and maintain her step so I wished her well and told her hopefully I would see her at the finishing line and asked her to have a drink or three waiting for me.

As I watched her torch light disappear in the distance, I felt lonely and at my lowest ebb. I really needed a drink. It was all I could think about. The light was fading but I could see the silhouette of somebody in front of me. I tried my hardest to catch her up. I needed some company to take my mind off dying of thirst. As I got nearer I realised this young lady was not alone.

"Come on, you can do it. Determination," she said to the two young men with her. She was a carer for people with mental disabilities and she was trying her hardest to encourage the men to continue with the walk. I got chatting to her and it certainly helped me, because before I knew it we were at the refreshment stage at Holme Pierrepont.

My legs felt as though they were on fire and my feet were starting to feel strangled by my trainers. They weren't leather and my feet were certainly suffering for it. The poor things hadn't been able to breathe for miles and I was literally plodding along now. What little grace I may have had at the beginning was now totally non-existent.

I grabbed my drink and I don't think I even tasted it. It was as though it dissolved as soon as it touched my lips. The young carer I had been walking with wished me luck as she boarded a minibus with her two young lads. I was in two minds whether to beg for a lift home! But I thought to myself: "Come on, Sylvia, you've come this far. Do something right and carry on." So I did.

Later on, I tagged on to a couple. I really couldn't face going the rest of the way on my own. I needed someone to lift my morale a little bit. Well, when I say a little, I mean heaps. I was introduced to the lady's brother who had been a long distance walker until recent years. Now he was disabled and walked doubled up in a severe stoop. His body also suffered spasmodic twitches. His courage started to make me feel ashamed. I was suffering from blisters on my feet and I thought my world was coming to an end. Yet, here was this man, barely able to control his walking into a rhythmic, easy motion, giving it all he had. I decided then that I was going to do this, blisters, aches, thirst and all.

The dark lanes seemed to go on forever and every part of the walk started to look the same. I felt as if I was chasing moonbeams. Well, perhaps stumbling after them would be more accurate.

"How far are we from RAF Newton?" I asked one of the

marshals. I was hoping he would say just around the corner, but that was wishful thinking.

"Ooh another five miles yet," he replied enthusiastically. Five miserable miles!

"Are you feeling it a bit?" he asked. That was an understatement. My toes were starting to chafe at the end of my trainers and every step I took became more and more agonising. My spine throbbed, in fact my whole body had a dull ache all over. I knew that I had perhaps bitten off more than I could chew this time.

I was desperately trying to keep my strength up both physically and mentally and I had just about come to the end of my tether. I knew that if I stopped and sat down I wouldn't get up again.

"Keep going, keep going, you have got to do it for yourself," I kept reminding myself. I had to. And when RAF Newton came into vision, it was a wonderful sight. I had achieved what I would have considered impossible 12 months earlier.

When I approached the gates I was swaying from side to side. I felt so drained. 'Welcome to RAF Newton', the sign said. Two air force marshals were at the gate to salute us and I asked how far it was to the reception.

"A hundred yards," came the reply.

My pace actually started to speed up. I wanted to get there but I could feel my body swaying even more. It was as though I had no control of it at all and I was turning to jelly. Two chaps came rushing over to me and said: "Put your arms in ours, love. We will help you along."

By this time I was smiling like a demented Cheshire cat. I was overwhelmed with what I had achieved and I wanted everyone to know. After I was given a most welcome drink, myself and a few other walkers were offered a lift back into the centre of Nottingham. Then I got a taxi home.

I was expecting the red carpet to be out when I got back. I should be so lucky! Stan was in bed, as were the boys. Well, it was half past four in the morning. But it was a pleasure for me to sit in my chair in the living room with a cup of tea and look back at my achievement. Well done, Sylvia, I said to myself. I would tell the others about it later and show them my wounds from the walk.

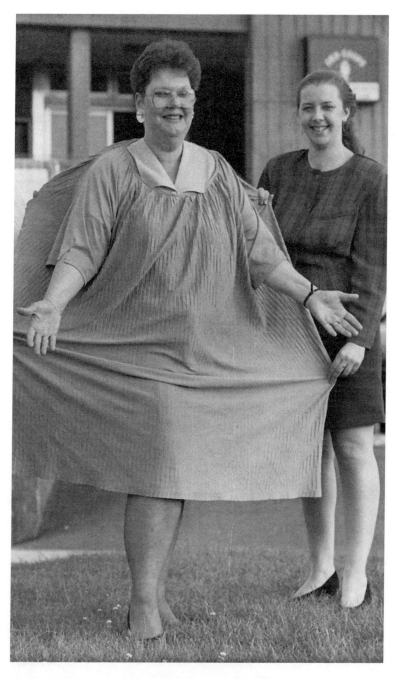

The weight comes off … but for how long?
Photograph by Simon Atkins for the Peterborough Evening Telegraph 1992

'Shame' © Sylvia Hurt

Chapter 23

One step forward, two steps back

Miracle cures, that's what they say.
Hypnosis works, that's what they say.
Handing money over with a promise of success.
They will make me regress to my painful past.
To realise the pain so it will never emerge again.
It cost me hundreds of pounds, I'm afraid to say.
I might as well have thrown my money away.

Some time later, I decided that I could improve my standard of living if I put our house on the market. It was logical to me that if I sold it, I would have collateral in the bank to the tune of £12,000 and I knew I would be able to put £13,000 on my next property. Life would be wonderful.

I managed to get myself a part-time job with the schools as an evening cleaner. Heather's welfare was my main concern. She wouldn't suffer if I worked at night.

It took me several years to sell my home. I had missed out on 12 properties due to the chain constantly collapsing. But in May 1992, I bought a lovely home just around the corner from my daughters which made life easier for us all.

I continued working until 8 August 1993, when I was walking our puppy over the surrounding fields and fell down a 12ft drop. It was an old railway siding. My injuries were so severe that I needed 13 screws and plates in my right ankle. Once again, I couldn't work and had to rely on benefit hand-outs which I found extremely hard.

I had put my life together but it had been shattered by sheer bad luck. The months went by and I started to gain so much weight that I could hardly move about under my own steam. I became angry again at my immobility and with Stan for seeming to enjoy the plight I was in. I started to eat foods straight out of the freezer and I wanted fats with everything. I was catching the bus into town and eating six Mars bars and six bags of crisps, then jacket potatoes with double helpings. I was on a roller coaster and just couldn't get off.

AM I NOT A PERSON?

I think Lisa had given up on me on this stage. She didn't comment on my size any more and she now accepts that I do have an eating disorder. It also became clear that Stan was deliberately catering for my needs all the time. He was in control of me and he knew that if I did conquer my terrible compulsion this would no longer be the case. This made me so angry. I was playing Stan's game but at the same time being destroyed by my inner torment, the silent world of abuse.

But because I couldn't walk far any more, I became more reliant on Stan again. Despite how I felt about him, at times he was my salvation at times. He would often roll me over in bed and ease my body up into a sitting position. But I knew Stan had abused me and at times my anger came to the surface.

"You're to blame for this!" I shouted in one of my angry outbursts. "You touched me when I was far too young!"

He replied: "But you had a lovely body, Sylv."

"So that gave you the right to touch me, did it?"

There was silence for a minute or two. He knew I was right. Stan eased my body up and I slowly shuffled to the top of the stairs. It was so painful, each step seemed to take minutes. I eventually made my way downstairs and eased my body into my chair, waiting for Stan to bring the cholesterol nightmare through to me.

I had a friend called Betty who constantly paid me compliments about my facial features. She was the only friend I had in Wollaton. Nobody else would speak to me. They treated me as if I was some sort of freak but Betty would bring me a grapefruit and try to encourage me with my weight. She knew nothing of my past.

I had heard a lot about hypnotherapy and I wondered whether this might be the answer. I knew that it was beyond my finances but if it was going to benefit me it was a small price to pay. I had spoken to Betty several times about it and she had offered to come along with me. She saw me as a normal person but society saw me as some sort of freak to be ridiculed.

After scanning the Yellow Pages, I managed to locate a practice and phoned up.

"I have a weight problem. Can you help?"

"Well, we have to know more details."

"I'm a survivor," I blurted out.

AM I NOT A PERSON?

"Survivor of what?" he enquired.

"Abuse, rejection ..." Our conversation continued and I made an appointment.

His surgery was in a posh suburb of Nottingham, two bus rides from my home. Betty had not let me down and had come along with me.

We arrived a few minutes early and after Bet had seen I was all right, she arranged to meet me at the pub around the corner. I was nervous, wondering if this man could help me. After a few minutes, I was shown into his plushly carpeted surgery which had a leather recliner seat. He did a few checks on my co-ordination then asked several questions to see if I was a suitable subject.

Then he said: "Right, Sylvia, let's get down to sorting you out".

It was what I had been waiting for ... a miracle cure. I took my coat off and he told me to sit in the recliner as he positioned the seat. Then he told me to lean back and look at the mural on the wall. It was a picture of rocks with the sea crashing against them.

As instructed, I closed my eyes and listened to the music. I could hear the waves hitting the rocks and for an instant I was on St Kilda beach where I was raped, but within seconds drifted off. I can't tell you anything else about it because the next thing I remember is being woken up.

"Do you feel relaxed, Sylvia?"

"Yes. Will this put me in control of my life and my eating?"

"Well, we can help you. You had a bad time at school. You weren't academically good."

I was immediately on the defensive. "I was. I was."

"Sylvia, I feel you need at least five sessions."

"What did you find out, then?"

"I'm afraid that's confidential."

I had just paid out £30 and this man wouldn't tell me what he had found, apart from saying that I was a dunce at school! But he still insisted he could help me and made another appointment for the following week.

The stupid thing was, I knew why I had this terrible compulsion. But here I was, looking for a miracle cure to eradicate all my pain. I said I would keep the appointment. But I didn't.

AM I NOT A PERSON?

I left the surgery to meet Betty.

"How did you get on, ducky?"

"I don't really know, I can't remember anything at all. I feel it's been a complete waste of time and money."

When I got home I didn't breathe a word to anyone and Betty was sworn to secrecy. Over a period of six months I tried many hypnotherapists, but in the end I felt I had thrown hundreds of pounds away. I even bought a Paul McKenna tape and for several weeks it was the best thing ever. Then I found I just couldn't listen to it anymore. I seemed to be rejecting the suggestions that were put into my brain.

One day, I was listening to the local radio station when I heard a voice that I recognised as the first therapist I had visited. It was a 'phone-in about hypnotherapy so I rang to ask why my brain wouldn't let me listen to the tape. I was on the air within seconds and I explained my problem to this man. He was sympathetic and arranged for me to 'phone his clinic so he could help. Within 30 minutes, he rang me back. "Why didn't you tell me I had seen you before?"

"Well, I didn't want the listeners to know we didn't have a successful outcome. But it's not your fault. I didn't keep my appointment because I knew that only I would be able to conquer my problem with food."

Chapter 24

The past, the present and the future

When I depart from this earth, I won't be hurt
But my family care.
How selfish of me to wallow in despair.
Life's for living, I instil in my mind,
But the food is always there

One summer's day in 1994 I yelled: "Stan, your breakfast is ready!"

It was usual for me to have to shout him to the table to eat his bacon, egg, tomatoes, and four slices of bread and butter with marmalade to finish. I was in control of my food intake on this particular day. I'd had bran flakes, skimmed milk and tea. I had opened the patio doors because, to me, to hear the birds singing was paradise.

As I gazed into the distance thinking about my chores for the day, Stan asked: "What's wrong Sylv?"

"Nothing, Stan," I said in a dream-like state, just relishing the tranquillity and the lovely morning breeze. As Stan wiped his bread 'round his plate, I supped the last dregs of my tea. I was in heaven. Then Stan got up and shut the patio doors.

"What have you done that for?" I yelled.

Then he locked the front door.

"No, Stan!" Clearly, his sexual gratification was on the agenda and his lust was in overdrive.

"When you say 'no', Sylv, you know you mean 'yes'."

Then he went upstairs and waited for me, but I stayed downstairs for as long as I could. Eventually, I had to go for a shower because I had an appointment in town. As the water soaked my body, I cried ... the abuse had never gone away and it was going to haunt me for the rest of my life.

I tried to compose myself while I washed my hair, hoping that Stan would not know that I had been crying. I didn't want him to see that he had affected me. But when I walked into the bedroom to dry my hair, he started on me again. I said 'no' to his advances over and over but it clearly didn't make any difference. He told me that as my husband he had every right to have sex when he wanted.

When he treated me like this, I became a little child again. I was paralysed by those eyes, those hands, those threats. The flashbacks were so vivid and I blamed Stan.

I was unable to fight off his lust and I just froze on the bed, my fists clenched and my teeth grinding, tension gripping my body. I was cocooned in the body and mind of a child in fear for her life and I was crying inside: "Why can't I stop it?"

I know that while Stan is with me, I will have pain all the time. He is now over 80 years old but Just the other day wanted to lie naked on my body. His behaviour is unacceptable to me and I now try to lead a separate life. I have my own bedroom but I face him day in, day out.

I can hear people saying: "Why do you put up with it?" and I'm sure many who have come this far in my story will not be able to fathom this out.

I have considered leaving so many times but why should I desert my family and leave my home? Also, my three children, who, I suppose, are in denial of the abuse I suffer, simply adore their father. Breaking up my family would only cause terrible pain to the ones I love most in this world. And I really couldn't face that.

*****

Writing this book has been a celebration for me. I have unburdened myself of the inner torment that has been festering away for all these years. I know deep down in my heart that survivors who read these words will be able to take the first step towards peeling away the layers of fear and being free.

True, my weight is still a major problem and every day is a battle with my compulsion. But I don't want to be thin. I just want to be allowed to live the life of a normal person.

I have managed to detach the blame from myself for my abuse, rejection, and mental cruelty thanks to a dear friend called Paul who has helped me enormously.

And Rape Crisis has been my lifeline for the past few years. They have supported me and helped me so much. Even when I was unable to get to the office, they would come to me. Without them, I definitely would not be where I am today.

AM I NOT A PERSON?

They see me as a normal person who has overcome so much in life and is battling with deep hurt and anger.

Because I am recognised as an intelligent human being who has struggled against abuse from various corners, I am now respected for my views. People value my opinion and I am often invited to talk to the caring professions in universities. I gladly accept, because what happened to my family must never happen again.

At some time in the future, I hope to become a foster carer and even have a place on a fostering panel. I believe people like me would be a valuable asset to this type of operation.

Despite the labels that were given to me and that have followed me through my life, I now own my house and drive my own car. I also paint and have produced several sculptures interpreting my pain. Not bad for someone who is 'sub-normal'.

One of my paintings hangs in the Nottingham University, where my friend is head of social studies. I want to thank her from the bottom of my heart for being one of the first to see me as a person rather than an obese person who should be pitied.

Today, if you'll excuse the clichés, the world is my oyster and my motto is 'Life is for living' and that is just what I aim to do.

And what of my children? Even though they have suffered plenty of pain and anger, they are all successful in their own fields. Mark is now a plasterer, Lisa is a team leader in an office, and Carl is a qualified electrician.

I'm also delighted to say that this generation has broken the cycle of abuse. So, for those who think that abused people always go on to abuse, it simply isn't true. I have never harmed my children and they have never harmed theirs.

I have been blessed with four gorgeous grandchildren and Lisa recently produced another boy. My darling Heather is now rapidly approaching her teens.

As for me, I may still battle every day with flashbacks and compulsive eating, but I will overcome.

And I now know one thing for certain.
I really do deserve to matter.

Appendix

1964
Letter from a Consultant Psychiatrist at Aston Hall to the Clerk to the Justices, City of Nottingham Juvenile Court

This girl ... gives a history of behaviour disturbance which she dates from her father's death in 1962, including running away from home, staying out late ... and trying to gas herself. There is also a history of running away from any difficulties, virtual unemployability and of telling a convincing story of her mother's death which appeared to be wishful thinking.

She has a very poor relationship with her mother, by whom she feels rejected ... she also gave an indication of other emotional problems not related to the mother.

Psychometric assessment has indicated that she is of dull-normal intelligence. On the standard, predominantly verbal tests her IQ was 90 but on a performance test her IQ was 73, this being not much above the level of sub-normality.

Her general behaviour here has been good but in a childish, dependent and apathetic kind of way. For a day or two, however, she showed disturbed behaviour of an hysterical type when she slouched in a chair, wept and would not speak or move without active persuasion ... although this type of behaviour does not cause much difficulty in a hospital setting I think it would be very difficult to cope with in the community.

Two days later
Probation Officer's report of investigation to the Nottingham City Juvenile Court

The warden of the hostel where Sylvia lived contacted me as she was concerned about her recent attitude to work and it would seem that she was continually changing her place of employment; combined with this it was said that her mother had died within the last week, Sylvia having been told of this by a neighbour when she went to visit her mother.

She was said to have returned to the hostel in a very shocked and distressed state and was so convincing about the matter that her story was not doubted.

Shortly after this she attempted to gas herself in her room at the hostel and was admitted to the General Hospital for a day or so.

On [date deleted] I was informed that there was no truth in the story of her mother's death and in view of all the circumstances she was obliged to leave the hostel and returned home with her mother.

As the situation between Sylvia and her mother has been incompatible, after discussion with [Sylvia's mother] I felt it was in the girl's best interests to bring her back to court as in the light of her

I

fabrication being discovered she may have attempted further injury to herself.

The matter of Sylvia being remanded to Aston Hall for observation by Dr ----- was discussed with [Sylvia's mother] who was in full agreement.

1966
To The Registrar, Mapperley Hospital
The above-named girl was under my supervision until [date deleted] ... having been brought before the court ... by her mother who deemed her beyond control.

This young woman is emotionally disturbed and I would be most grateful if she could be seen by a psychiatrist at his earliest convenience.

Sylvia's great trouble is failure to maintain employment. She has been placed in two residential jobs of her own choice but left both after about three months. She has worked in factories, but dislikes this type of employment.

At the moment she is unemployed ... she is drifting around aimlessly and appears in a very confused state of mind. Her present intentions are to leave Nottingham without any idea of where she will go or how she will get there.

Thank you for your help in this matter.

Mrs Barton [name changed]
Probation Officer

Later the same year
Dear Dr -----
Further to our telephone conversation with you ... concerning this young woman, I enclose an old report to give you some idea of the family background, also a copy of my letter to Mapperley Hospital [earlier] this year.

Sylvia was referred to me yesterday by the City Police as she had been roaming around the streets in the early hours of Sunday morning, but her story is that an uncle took her to Police Headquarters because she refused to go home to her mother.

I will see that she keeps her appointment with you ... and thank you for your help in this matter.

Mrs Barton
Probation Officer

Dear Mrs Barton
For the completion of your records I confirm that I examined the above-named and that I did not find that any psychiatric action is indicated. She is an aimless, feckless person who reacts to everything with a feeling of being 'fed up'. She does not like anything or anybody, she does not like her family, her job, her lodgings, and she

spends her time aimlessly wandering about. She works only very spasmodically and when her means run out she seeks the help of the National Assistance Board. She has no goal or interest in life and seems unable to form lasting human relationships. She is essentially inco-operative [sic]. She is not suitable for any form of psychiatric assistance. At the same time, she is not a delinquent and compulsory admission to an educational institution is not possible.

Yours sincerely

Dr -----

1976
From a Consultant Psychiatrist to the children's department at St Ann's Hospital

The mother first came to our notice some three years ago since when she has frequently been admitted to Mapperley and St Ann's hospitals exhibiting the most severe and violent type of hysterical dissociation. This has been of such severity on occasions that we have had to resort to ECT to break the pattern of violence which she has exhibited, particularly towards the nursing staff.

During the whole of this time the children have, of course, been much affected by the mother's behaviour ... I would not have become involved in this except that [the] mother had [one of the children] with her on her last visit ... [the child's] restlessness and complete lack of concern for her instruction and her mounting irritability ... made me think that this was a situation which merits some expert assessment.

1977
From a senior social worker to the Clerk to the County Council

Mrs ----- [the foster parent] rang to discuss with me the problems relating to the children seeing their mother. She is aware that [the other social worker] and colleagues at Mapperley Hospital have insisted that the mother has no contact with the children, either by visit or by telephone.

However, this is causing the children considerable distress as they have now had no contact for almost a month. Apparently, their father does visit but the mother, although she is now out of hospital, has so far been unable to see them.

Mrs ----- naturally appreciates that there are reasons behind this decision but the children are getting more and more distressed about not seeing mother.

Normally, Mr and Mrs ----- can pacify children in this situation but on this occasion they are not able to do so, especially Lisa. She feels the children have genuine love for their mother and are beginning to wonder if there is any deep reason why they have not seen their mother. Last weekend they bought a present for their mother but are not able to give it to her.

27 days later
Arranged for Sylvia and Stan to visit the children and for she and I to pick the children up and take them home for tea - the first step in a gradual process of rehabilitation.

1978
Since 1977, the children have remained at home continuously with their mother ... throughout this period I have been entirely satisfied that it is in the children's best interests to remain at home in the care of their mother.

During the past 12 months Sylvia has had several periods of mild depression, usually at times when she has financial difficulties, but at no time has she become suicidal and nor has she become excitable and aggressive, and it has not been necessary to consider admitting her to hospital.

I have discussed the situation with Dr ----- who feels that Sylvia's mental state has stabilised to some extent now that her husband has disappeared off the scene. I agree with this and also feel that the knowledge that we are able to remove the children if she is not providing adequate care for them at home, combined with her positive and co-operative relationship with myself, has motivated her to make more effort to overcome minor difficulties of the sort which precipitated hospital admissions in the past.

Financial problems have been the biggest difficulty in the family during the past year ... Mr Hurt informed the DHSS that he was now living with Sylvia and his children on a permanent basis and wished to take on the responsibility of maintaining the family and Sylvia's entitlement to supplementary benefit therefore ended. However, Mr Hurt earns only a very low wage and he never seemed to be able to nor really motivated to maintain the family properly. The children were always adequately fed and clothed but fuel bills etc were never paid on time and Sylvia found this increasingly worrying.

... I have taken a close interest in [the children's] progress at school. At no time have the children's schools felt at all anxious about their welfare. Lisa is a very able child and the quantity and quality of her school work is quite remarkable. Her behaviour at school is exceptionally good and her teacher describes her as pleasant, friendly, co-operative, helpful etc. [Mark's teacher] also describes him as friendly, helpful and hard-working. Carl has made an excellent start at school ... and can already read fluently at the age of six. The fact that the children are making good progress in school and exhibit no behaviour problems whatsoever confirms my feelings that, although their home-life is sometimes a bit haphazard, they are in not any way being emotionally damaged by remaining at home.

There is no doubt whatsoever that the children themselves wish to remain at home with their mother. They are very frightened by the idea of having to leave home again.

Useful information

The Rape Crisis Centre in Nottingham is on:
0115 941 0440

Numbers for all other RC centres can be obtained by calling
the Rape Crisis Federation on:
0161 272 7005

They are also listed on the 'Am I Not A Person?' web site:
http://www.thewordfactory.co.uk/person

and on the Compuserve site:
http://ourworld.compuserve.com/homepages/theword_factory

The NSPCC contact details are:
Tel: 0800 800 500
e-mail: helpline@nspcc.org.uk
web site: http://www.nspcc.org.uk

ChildLine UK contact details are:
ChildLine, Freepost 1111, London N1 0BR
Tel: 0800 1111
web site: http://www.childline.org.uk

The Child Abuse Survivors Network is at:
PO Box 1, London N1 7SN

Sylvia Hurt can be contacted at:
The Word Factory, Syntax House,
PO Box 186, Nottingham NG11 6DU
Please put Sylvia's name on the envelope and
mark it 'Private and Confidential'.

If you want to e-mail Sylvia Hurt in total
confidence, send your message to:
sylvia-hurt@thewordfactory.co.uk

Sylvia will not reply to your message unless
you expressly request her to do so. Your e-mail
details will not be held on any computer.

A Portrayal of Pain

Sylvia Hurt has written poems expressing her pain and has produced paintings which depict in graphic detail the mental and physical torture that is sexual abuse.

Building on the success of 'Am I Not A Person?', The Word Factory will be publishing a collection of these poems and full-colour paintings entitled 'A Portrayal of Pain' [SSP £6.99].

If you would like to receive an early print of this book, please send your details to:
The Word Factory, Syntax House,
PO Box 186, Nottingham NG11 6DU
e-mail: portrayal@thewordfactory.co.uk